100 HEALTH-BOOSTING
FOODS

100 HEALTH-BOOSTING FOODS

facts and recipes for super health

hamlyn

An Hachette UK company
www.hachette.co.uk

First published in Great Britain in 2007
by Hamlyn, a division of Octopus
Publishing Group Ltd
Endeavour House
189 Shaftesbury Avenue
London WC2H 8JY
www.octopusbooksusa.com

This edition published in 2015

Distributed in the US by
Hachette Book Group
1290 Avenue of the Americas
4th and 5th Floors
New York, NY 10020

Distributed in Canada by
Canadian Manda Group
664 Annette Street
Toronto, Ontario, Canada M6S 2C8

ISBN 978-0-60063-003-6

Printed and bound in China

10 9 8 7 6 5 4 3 2 1

Notes

Ovens should be preheated to the specified temperature.
If using a convection oven, follow the manufacturer's instructions
for adjusting the time and temperature. Broilers should also
be preheated.

This book includes dishes made with nuts and nut derivatives.
It is advisable for those with known allergic reactions to nuts and
nut derivatives and those who may be potentially vulnerable to
these allergies, such as pregnant and nursing mothers, invalids,
the elderly, babies, and children, to avoid dishes made with nuts
and nut oils. It is also prudent to check the labels of already-
prepared ingredients for the possible inclusion of nut derivatives.

The U. S. Food and Drug Administration advises that eggs should
not be consumed raw. This book contains some dishes made with
raw or lightly cooked eggs. It is prudent for more vulnerable
people, such as pregnant and nursing mothers, invalids, the
elderly, babies, and young children, to avoid uncooked or slightly
cooked dishes made with eggs.

Meat and poultry should be cooked thoroughly. To test if poultry is
cooked, pierce the flesh through the thickest part with a skewer or
fork—the juices should run clear, never pink or red.

Safety note

This book should not be considered a replacement for professional
medical treatment; a physician should be consulted on all matters
relating to health. While the advice and information in this book is
believed to be accurate, neither the author nor publisher can
accept any legal responsibility for any injury or illness sustained
while following it.

Note on nutritional information in this book

Nutritional experts measure foods and their components in
grams and milliliters because these metric units provide the most
accurate measurements. These units have been used in this book
to provide the most accurate analysis of the nutritional contents of
the foods listed. For further information on the average serving
size of each food, refer to Nutritive Value of Foods, a free
publication by the United States Department of Agriculture, which
can be found at: www.ars.usda.gov/services/docs.htm?docid=6282.

contents

6

introduction

The very fact that you're reading this book shows that you are interested in your health or that of your loved ones. It is certainly a subject that should concern all of us; time and again scientific research has linked diets rich in certain foods with better health and the absence of particular diseases. For example, the low incidence of serious disease among Mediterranean populations is attributed to specific foods in their diet (seafood, tomatoes, olive oil, and red wine).

Since most of us choose what we eat we are, to some extent, responsible for our own health. We need a balanced diet that provides all of the necessary vitamins, minerals, protein, carbohydrates, fiber and fats to maintain our health and well-being. You may be tired of hearing the phrase "you are what you eat" but it accurately reflects the fact that our food does more than just satisfy pangs of hunger. It helps the body grow, repair, and regenerate cells; function efficiently and fight

off infection. It, therefore, makes sense to choose the best foods possible for the purpose, foods that are rich in nutrients and have been linked with specific health benefits.

What are health-boosting foods?

Currently, there is a great deal of interest in the health-boosting properties of certain foods, often referred to as "super foods," or "miracle foods." Ongoing research studies and scientific analysis have shown the specific health benefits of certain foods. For example, cruciferous vegetables, such as broccoli and cabbage, have been strongly linked with a decreased risk of cancer, while oily fish is believed to help protect against heart disease.

This book concentrates on 100 top foods that can help boost your health. These foods work in various ways, depending on their specific composition of nutrients and phytonutrients (chemicals derived from plants). Many contain antioxidants, beneficial nutrients that help protect against infections and diseases and slow down the aging processes in the body.

Besides promoting good general health, some of the health-boosting foods in this book are particularly important for tackling specific conditions—for example, insomnia and high blood pressure. Some are very important for people who are stressed; others make you look better, improving the appearance of skin and complexion, and strengthening teeth and nails.

Boosting your well-being

You don't need to become obsessive about your health, but knowing which foods are health boosters can help you make good choices. Doing the best you can for your health by regularly eating foods that provide good-quality fuel for your body has other benefits. It can make you feel good from within and more optimistic in general. It should also give you more energy and take away the sluggishness caused by too much junk food.

7

eating your way to health

10

healthy eating

Experts believe that many of the ailments found by modern industrialized western societies are due to diet and lack of regular physical activity. This book focuses on the nutrient-rich foods you should be eating, but, on the subject of physical activity, most of us probably need to increase the amount we do. Simply walking more every day, instead of using cars, escalators, and elevators, is a good start. Also, try to make exercise a routine part of life instead of an occasional extra.

Good nutrition

The importance of good nutrition—at all stages of our lives—cannot be overemphasized. It lies at the very heart of good health, since the cells in our bodies, essentially the body's building blocks, rely on a good supply of nutrients in the diet to create and continually renew all the tissue and organs in the body. The *essential* nutrients required by our bodies are carbohydrates, protein, fats, vitamins, and minerals (phytonutrients—see page 24—are a bonus). Without the vital nutrients cellular health, and, therefore, general health, is adversely affected because cells that function inefficiently result in low energy levels, premature aging, and disease.

Variety

Apart from human milk, which alone provides for a baby's needs in the first few months of life, there is no one food that provides all the nutrients our bodies need. However nutrient-rich it may be, eating loads of just one type of food is rarely good for us. On the contrary, we need to eat a wide variety of foods, from all of the main food groups (see below), to benefit from all of the different nutrients available. In addition, different nutrients tend to interact and work in synergy. For example, Vitamins C and E actually work together to make each other more effective—vitamin C recycles vitamin E, allowing it to carry on working longer.

Thinking ahead

What you eat has a huge impact on your health. It affects the way that you feel and look, how much energy you have, and how healthy you are overall, not only now but longer term, too. A poor diet—and therefore, poor cell function—will affect your future health. This aspect should not be ignored because, thanks largely to modern medicine and improvements in hygiene, most of us can expect to enjoy much longer life spans than earlier generations. Since we are likely to live longer, let's enjoy those years in as good health as possible. We need to do all we possibly can to protect ourselves from the physical consequences of aging. In practice, this means looking at what we eat and drink and evaluating how our diets could be changed to meet our bodies' needs now and in the future.

A healthy balance

A healthy diet is primarily about balance. Our bodies need certain amounts of carbohydrates, proteins, fats, vitamins, and minerals in order to function efficiently and, by eating sensibly, this can easily be achieved. With busy lifestyles and stressful jobs, it is all too easy to neglect our diets. But bear in mind that a balanced diet will boost health, energy, and vitality and doesn't necessarily mean hours of preparation and cooking (see "Shopping wisely," page 33).

The simplest way to ensure you are eating a nutritionally

sound diet is to eat a wide variety of foods and to think of your food intake in terms of a plate containing foods from each of the five major food groups in varying proportions. Although many foods contain all the various different nutrients to some extent, some foods are predominantly carbohydrate, protein, or fat, and are relatively easily recognized as such (see pages 14–19).

Bread, cereals, and potatoes

This group of starchy carbohydrate foods is the major source of energy in the diet and should make up the biggest portion on your plate. The group includes whole-grain cereals, bread, pasta, rice, potatoes, and yams. All the foods in this group are low in fat and high in starchy carbohydrates and dietary fiber.

Fruits and vegetables

These should make up the next biggest portion on your plate. Fruits and vegetables are low in fat, high in dietary fiber and rich in vitamins, minerals, and other plant chemicals, which are believed to play an important part in preventing many common illnesses, such as heart disease, diabetes, and cancer.

The food pyramid

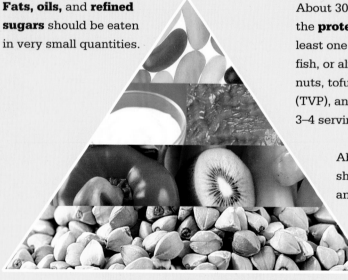

Fats, oils, and **refined sugars** should be eaten in very small quantities.

About 30% of your diet should come from the **protein** and **healthy fats** group. At least one meal a day should contain meat, fish, or alternatives, such as legumes, nuts, tofu, textured vegetable protein (TVP), and beans. You should also include 3–4 servings of **dairy produce** a day.

About 30% of your diet should be made up of **fruits** and **vegetables.**

About 40% of your diet should be made up of **breads, cereals, and pasta.**

Dairy foods

Milk, cheese, yogurt, and other dairy products should make up the third largest portion on your plate—choose low-fat dairy products to avoid too high an intake of fat. Milk and dairy foods supply our bodies with protein, calcium and zinc, and vitamins B_{12}, B_2, A and D.

Meat, fish and alternatives

Protein foods—lean meat, poultry, fish, lentils, legumes, eggs, soy products, nuts, and seeds—should make up the fourth largest portion on your plate. Many of these foods are also good sources of B vitamins and minerals, such as iron, calcium, magnesium, and zinc.

Fats and sugars

Foods containing fats and/or refined carbohydrate, such as sugar and honey, should take up the least space on the plate. Such foods include margarine, butter, cooking oils, oil-based dressings, ice cream, pastries, cookies, confectionery, and soft drinks. Some fat is essential in the diet, but too much can lead to heart disease and obesity. Sugars provide calories yet very few nutrients, and too much sugar can result in weight gain and tooth decay.

Top tips for healthy eating

Healthy eating does not mean cutting out sugary or fatty snacks completely, it simply means achieving the correct balance in your diet, being aware of the food that you eat and following a few simple guidelines:

- Eat a variety of foods
- Maintain a healthy weight
- Always refuse second helpings if you need to watch your weight
- Eat plenty of fruits and vegetables and foods rich in starch and fiber
- Choose foods that are low in fat
- Restrict your use of salt and sugar in cooking and at the table
- Eat small meals and healthy snacks throughout the day (known as "grazing"), instead of eating two or three large meals
- Eat only when you are hungry, instead of for the sake of it
- Never go food shopping when you are hungry
- Don't buy the foods you find hard to resist. That way there will be no temptation in the cupboards at home
- Drink alcohol only in moderation.

13

14
carbohydrates

Carbohydrate foods provide the energy the body needs to function, both physically and mentally. There are two types of carbohydrate: sugars and starches, formerly known as "simple" and "complex" carbohydrates, respectively. Typical sources of carbohydrate are grains, legumes, vegetables, and fruits.

Starches versus sugars

Starchy foods are much better energy providers than sugary ones. Starchy foods include grains and their products, such as bread, pasta, and breakfast cereals, and starchy vegetables such as potatoes. Simple sugars are those found naturally in milk, fruits, and some vegetables. Refined white sugar contains calories yet no nutrients and is, therefore, of no nutritious value at all.

Starchy carbohydrates with a high fiber content—for example legumes and unrefined whole-grain foods that have lost nothing during their processing—are particularly good for you because high-fiber carbohydrates are digested at a slower rate. As a result, the blood sugar level in the body doesn't rise as quickly, whereas low-fiber carbohydrates are digested more quickly and consequently raise blood sugar rapidly. Rapid rises in blood sugar are undesirable since they cause the body to produce increased levels of insulin, the

hormone that helps regulate blood sugar levels. Over time, this can result in health problems such as diabetes.

The effect of different foods on blood-sugar levels is now better understood. Common foods are ranked according to the glycemic index (GI) where 0 is good and 100 (refined sugar) is bad.

The other major advantages of starchy foods is that their bulkiness gives a feeling of fullness when eaten (particularly useful for dieters) and the slow release of their carbohydrate helps to sustain energy over a long period of time. For this reason, sports people usually eat a very starchy meal hours before competing as an effective way of storing energy for slow release, for example, during a long, grueling running marathon or a bicycle race.

Which are starchy foods?

Starchy foods include all types of true grains (wheat, oats, rye, barley, millet, corn) and similar foods, such as buckwheat, quinoa, and rice; products made from them, such as bread, tortillas, pasta, noodles, couscous, cornmeal, and breakfast cereals; plus the starchy vegetables, such as potatoes, peas, yams, and plantain.

Many of these foods, particularly the whole-grain cereals, are valuable sources of important vitamins and minerals, and many of them also contribute to the protein content of the diet.

Fiber

Plenty of dietary fiber (also called roughage) in the diet is important for slowing the release of sugars into the bloodstream; it also keeps the bowel healthily active (see "Grains and legumes," page 28).

The best sources are whole-grain cereal foods, such as whole-grain bread, whole-grain pasta, and brown rice. Vegetables and legumes (chickpeas, beans, and lentils) are very good sources of fiber, and seeds and fruits (especially pears, prunes, figs, and raspberries) also make an important contribution.

How much?

Nutritionists recommend that a high percentage—40–50 percent—of our daily calorie intake should come from unrefined carbohydrates.

To increase your intake of high-fiber carbohydrates, replace white bread, white rice, and sugary breakfast cereal with unrefined versions—whole-grain bread, brown rice, rolled oats, bran flakes, and whole-wheat pasta. In addition, snack on dried fruits and use legumes as a base for hearty soups and stews.

16

proteins

Proteins are the basic building blocks that are found in all cells in our bodies. They make up the structure of the cells, as well as the elements inside, including enzymes and hormones. These structural elements are constantly being worn out so they need to be replaced by new proteins from our food.

What are proteins?

Proteins, found mainly in meat, fish, eggs, dairy products, grains, beans, peas, lentils, and soy products, are made up of chains of amino acids. There are about 20 different amino acids, and the order in which they are linked in the chain depends on the type of protein they are making, be it a grain of wheat or muscle tissue in a cow. When we digest and absorb these foods, the chains are broken down into the individual amino acids. Our bodies then build up new chains with the amino acids in the right order to form different parts of the human body, such as hair, muscle, or a hormone.

Vegetable versus animal protein

It used to be thought that proteins from vegetable sources, such as grains and beans, were of a lower quality than those from animal sources, such as meat and eggs, but it has since been shown that this is not true. They do have less protein per unit weight than meat products but the quality is the same. Overall, vegetable proteins, such as bread, pasta, beans, and lentils, are a healthier option because vegetables and grains contain more fiber and a lot less fat than animal protein foods such as meat, cheese, and milk.

Dairy products

Milk, yogurt, cheese, and other dairy products are good sources of protein and provide essential minerals and vitamins. Milk is an important source of calcium and also of the B vitamin riboflavin. With the exception of children under two years, who need whole milk for their development, most of us should use low-fat dairy products. Much of the content of fat-soluble vitamins (A, D, E) is lost, but the essential minerals, such as calcium, are still available.

Why do we need proteins?

Every cell in our bodies is partly composed of protein. We need adequate supplies of protein to build cells and for the existing cells to go through their continuous process of growing and replacing themselves. We need to eat protein every day because our bodies can't store it—you cannot stock up on protein by eating large amounts of it once a week. As well as their role as building blocks, proteins, like carbohydrates, supply us with energy to fuel our bodies.

To compare, 1 gram of protein supplies 4 calories, whereas 1 gram of carbohydrate supplies 3.5 calories and 1 g of fat supplies 9 calories. If we are low on energy, our bodies will use proteins for fuel first, but this is like fueling a furnace with paper money, since, unlike fats and carbohydrates, proteins have a much more important structural role, too.

The recommended protein intake in the diet is about 10 percent of the total calories consumed.

17

18

fats

Our bodies need some fat for energy, internal processes, and for the fat-soluble vitamins (vitamins A, D, E, and K). The body can make all the fatty acids it requires, except for the so-called essential fatty acids, which must be acquired from the diet. However, all fats are high in calories, so it's advisable to restrict the total amount of fat in the diet to maintain a healthy weight as well as to control unhealthy blood cholesterol levels.

Cholesterol

This is a natural and necessary form of fat manufactured in the body from dietary fats. There are two types: "good" cholesterol (high-density lipoprotein, HDL) and "bad" cholesterol (low-density lipoprotein, LDL). Too much of the latter can clog the arteries, leading to heart disease and strokes. High levels of blood cholesterol may be reduced by restricting fat in the diet, especially saturated fat.

The different types of fat

The prime sources of fat in our diets are dairy products, meat, oils, and fried foods. The main types of fat are saturated fats, trans fats, monounsaturated fats, and polyunsaturated fats.

Saturated and trans fats

Usually solid at room temperature, saturated fats come mostly from animal sources—the fat on meat, butter, lard, cream, and cheese—although vegetable sources include coconut butter and palm oil. A high concentration of saturated fat in the diet raises blood cholesterol levels, increasing the risk of blocked arteries, stroke, and heart disease.

The process of hardening vegetable oil to make margarine is called hydrogenation and results in the production of trans fats. Trans fats are the worst fat of all for the heart and have been linked with an increased risk of breast cancer. They are also particularly harmful to diabetics because they interfere with insulin receptors responsible for control of blood sugar.

High quantities of saturated fats and trans fats are found in many fast foods as well as in processed foods, such as cookies, cakes, and pastries.

Eating less fat

- **Choose lower-fat versions of dairy products, such as skimmed and semi-skimmed milk and reduced-fat cheese**
- **Use less fat in cooking. Broil and bake instead of frying and roasting**
- **Opt for low-fat spreads**
- **Use lean cuts of meat and remove the skin from poultry.**

Monounsaturated fats

Olive oil, rapeseed oil, avocados, and many nuts are sources of monounsaturated fat. These fats help maintain healthy cholesterol levels and are thought to protect against heart disease.

Polyunsaturated fats

These fats include the essential fatty acids (omega-3 and omega-6 fats) our bodies require from our diet, and they help decrease the harmful LDL cholesterol level in blood. Good sources are fresh nuts and seeds and their oils (such as sunflower and walnut oils), leafy green vegetables, seafood, and oily fish. Essential fatty acids should account for at least 15 percent of our calorie intake. Most people get plenty of omega-6 fats in their diet (due to the widespread use of polyunsaturated oils) but need to focus on consuming more omega-3s.

Everyday fats

Butter and margarine have the same calorie content, whether or not the margarine is marked "polyunsaturated." Butter is a good source of the fat-soluble vitamins A and D, which are added to margarine. Low-fat spreads have a high water content, therefore, a lower calorie content than butter or margarine. Most low-fat spreads have added fat-soluble vitamins.

Most cheeses have a high fat content. Quark is low in fat, as is low-fat ricotta. Heavy cream is 50 percent fat.

19

vitamins

There are two main types of vitamins—fat-soluble and water-soluble ones. The fat-soluble vitamins, A, D, E, and K, are stored in the body, and taking excessive amounts of them could be harmful. The water-soluble vitamins, vitamin C and the B complex vitamins, are not stored in the body and are, therefore, needed in the diet every day. Any excess amounts of these are excreted in the urine.

Vitamin A and beta-carotene

An antioxidant, vitamin A is essential for vision in dim light and for the maintenance of healthy skin and surface tissues. It is stored in the liver and is toxic in excessive amounts. Vitamin A is found in cheese, eggs, whole milk, and butter, and liver has a very high content.

Vitamin A can also be made in the body from beta-carotene (often referred to as its precursor), which is found in leafy green vegetables and in orange-colored fruits and vegetables, such as carrots and apricots.

Vitamin D

Vitamin D is essential for maintaining healthy levels of calcium and phosphorus in the body and for building healthy bones and teeth.

Deficiency causes rickets in children and osteomalacia (bone thinning) in adults.

The body makes its own vitamin D through the action of sunlight on the skin. Dietary sources are of less importance, except for people who cannot go out or who do not expose their skin to the light. Sources include oily fish, milk, butter, and egg yolks. Vitamin D is added to margarine, and some breakfast cereals and yogurts.

Vitamin E

One of the top antioxidants, Vitamin E fights free radicals (see page 24) and helps skin stay healthy. It is found in poultry, fish, vegetables, vegetable oils, wheat germ, nuts, and seeds.

Vitamin K

Vitamin K helps the body to make a number of proteins, one of which is necessary for blood clotting. It also helps prevent osteoporosis. It is found in leafy green vegetables, soy oil, and margarine.

The B vitamins

The vitamin B complex comprises eight vitamins: thiamin (B_1), riboflavin (B_2), niacin (B_3), pantothenic acid (B_5), pyridoxine (B_6), cobalamins (B_{12}), biotin, and folate (also known as folic acid).

Some of the B vitamins are essential for the release of energy from the food we eat; others are involved in making cells—some make nerve cells, which is why a deficiency of certain B vitamins may result in depression. B_6, B_{12}, and folate make red blood cells. These three also help protect the heart via their action on homocysteine, while folate helps protect unborn babies against spina bifida.

The B vitamins are widely distributed in foods, including meat, milk, organ meat, fish, eggs, vegetables, fruits, and whole grains. Many breakfast cereals are fortified with B vitamins.

Vitamin C

Another antioxidant, vitamin C, is needed for the growth and maintenance of healthy connective tissue, for boosting immunity, and for helping the body absorb iron.

For humans, vitamin C must come from the diet. The best sources are certain fruits, particularly black currants, strawberries, kiwi fruit, guavas, and citrus fruits. Green salads and vegetables are also useful, particularly potatoes, because of the large quantities generally eaten.

Vitamin C in fruits and vegetables diminishes with storing and cooking. Frozen vegetables may, therefore, sometimes have a higher vitamin C content than fresh vegetables that have been stored for some time.

Vitamin and mineral requirements

The amount of each vitamin and mineral we need changes according to our age, health, gender, and level of activity.

- **Children generally need more vitamins because they are growing and active**
- **Pregnant women are advised to take supplements of folate in the first twelve weeks of pregnancy**
- **People over the age of 50 generally become less active so need less energy. It is, therefore, important that the food that they eat is more nutrient-dense than the average diet.**

22

minerals

Our bodies need minerals in the diet for the growth and maintenance of bones, cells, and tissues. Some minerals—for example, zinc, iron, and chromium—are needed in only small quantities and are called trace minerals; others are required in much larger amounts. The more important dietary minerals are calcium, iron, and zinc. Phosphorus and magnesium are also important, but a diet that provides sufficient calcium will also provide adequate phosphorus and magnesium.

Calcium

People of all ages, not just children, need calcium because it is vital for forming and continually strengthening bones and teeth. Calcium and phosphorus together form the framework of the skeleton. A deficiency of calcium may result in osteoporosis in later life, where calcium is lost from the bone, making it painful to bear weight. To prevent osteoporosis, it is important to build strong bones early in life, when the bones are growing actively, through weight-bearing exercise and adequate dietary calcium.

Probably the most widely available sources of dietary calcium are milk, cheese, and yogurt. Because the calcium in milk is in the watery part of the liquids, using skimmed or semi-skimmed milk, or low-fat yogurts and cheeses, does not reduce calcium intake. Butter and cream contain little calcium. Calcium is also naturally available in other foods, such as kale, tinned sardines, almonds, and sesame seeds, and is often added to white bread, soy milk, and tofu.

In addition to strengthening bones and teeth, calcium acts as a natural tranquilizer, soothing irritability and aiding insomnia.

Other dietary minerals

- **Chromium (trace mineral):** Works with insulin to balance blood sugar levels, helps lower cholesterol levels, and protect against heart disease
- **Copper (trace mineral):** Helps the body use iron and convert food to energy
- **Fluoride (trace mineral):** Helps protect teeth
- **Iodine (trace mineral):** Helps control metabolic activity
- **Magnesium:** Helps cells and muscles work efficiently. Helps the body use calcium and potassium
- **Manganese (trace mineral):** An antioxidant and important for bone structure and nerve function
- **Phosphorus:** Required for healthy cells, bones, and teeth
- **Potassium:** Helps in cellular growth and controlling blood pressure. Also good for the nervous system and for regulating bodily fluids and the acid–alkali balance in the body. Required for muscle activity and helps prevent cramp
- **Selenium (trace mineral):** A major antioxidant (see page 24) with anti-cancer powers
- **Sodium:** Helps regulate the body's water content and enables the nerves to function effectively.

Iron

Iron is particularly important for the formation of hemoglobin, the red pigment in blood. In theory, we are born with enough iron to last throughout life, however, if enough dietary iron is not eaten to restore any losses, anemia can result.

The best sources of iron in the diet are red meat and liver because iron from these sources, is most easily absorbed. The iron in eggs is also well absorbed, but the iron in vegetables or added to flour is less well absorbed. Consuming a source of vitamin C, such as orange juice, with an iron-rich food helps the body absorb the iron. Tea inhibits absorption of iron, so avoid drinking it around meal times.

Zinc

An antioxidant (see page 24), zinc is a trace mineral that helps in the healing of wounds, is involved in enzyme activity, and is essential for healthy sex organs and male reproduction. It is present in a variety of foods—meat and dairy foods are good sources, as are nuts, whole grains, and seeds.

24

phytonutrients

Phytonutrients, which are also known as phytochemicals, are naturally occurring chemicals derived from plants. Unlike true nutrients (see pages 14–23), phytonutrients are not necessary for sustaining life, but they are believed to actively help prevent ill health or diseases. They are particularly associated with preventing and/or treating cancer, heart disease, diabetes, and high blood pressure.

Antioxidants

Antioxidants are powerful protective chemical compounds, which slow the rate of damaging oxidation in the body caused by free radicals. Free radicals are unstable oxygen molecules in our bodies generated by pollution, sunlight, cigarettes, certain foods, stress, and normal metabolic processes, such as breathing. Free radicals destabilize other, healthy molecules, initiating a chain reaction of cellular destruction and DNA degradation, resulting in accelerated aging and degenerative conditions and diseases such as cataracts, atherosclerosis, and cancer.

Uncooked fresh fruits and vegetables and most legumes are the best sources for antioxidants. Others include tea, red wine, olive oil, dark chocolate, and many grains.

Useful phytonutrients

Flavonoids such as quercetin and ellagic acid and resveratrol (found in grapes and wine). Usually antioxidant, sometimes anti-inflammatory, sometimes antibiotic, flavonoids have potent anticarcinogenic properties. Some work by preventing cancer-promoting estrogen from getting into cells, others suppress COX-2 (cyclooxygenase), an enzyme that enables cancer to grow and spread.

Anthocyanidins a class of flavonoids with powerful antioxidant properties and thought to be 50 times more powerful than vitamin E. Abundant in red, purple, and blue fruits, especially berries.

Carotenoids such as alphacarotene, betacarotene, lycopene, lutein, zeaxanthin. Powerful antioxidants with anticancer and anti-ageing properties.

Glucosinolates such as isothiocyanates, sulforaphane, indoles. Anticancer compounds found in cruciferous vegetables.

How do antioxidants help us?

Eating antioxidant-rich foods helps prevent ill health as the antioxidants disarm the unstable molecules—slowing down, preventing, or even reversing diseases resulting from cellular damage. Cancer cells, for example, are essentially normal cells that contain DNA damaged by free radicals. Because antioxidants stop free radicals and reduce DNA damage, they are a major defense against cancer.

As well as protecting us against serious degenerative diseases, antioxidants also boost the immune system, help prevent minor infections, reduce inflammation, and help protect against conditions associated with premature aging such as skin wrinkling and memory loss.

Variety offers protection

There are over 4,000 different antioxidants— the key ones are vitamins A, C, and E. The minerals selenium, manganese, and zinc, some of the B vitamins and certain enzymes and amino acids also have antioxidant properties. Some antioxidants operate in water-soluble parts of the body, while others work in the fatty areas of cells and tissues. Some are better at fighting certain free radicals than others. A varied diet containing plenty of different antioxidant foods is, therefore, the best way to boost health, and why we should eat at least five portions of fruits and vegetables every day.

Top-scoring antioxidant foods

Using test-tube analysis, researchers from the Human Nutrition Research Center on Aging, Tufts University, Boston, Massachusetts, have rated foods according to their ability to quench damaging oxygen-free radicals, known as Oxygen Radical Absorbance Capacity. ORAC values are given as units per (3½ ounces) food.

Prunes	5,770
Pomegranates	3,037
Raisins	2,830
Blueberries	2,400
Blackberries	2,036
Garlic	1,940
Kale	1,770
Strawberries	1,540
Spinach	1,260
Raspberries	1,220
Brussels sprouts	980
Plums	949
Alfalfa sprouts	930
Broccoli florets	890
Beets	840
Oranges	750
Red grapes	739
Red bell peppers	710
Cherries	670
Kiwifruits	602

health-boosting foods at a glance

Now that you know about all the different nutrients your body needs and how phytonutrients can boost health, you can start discovering which foods are the most nutritious. Health-boosting foods possess a high level of nutrients compared with their number of calories. The following pages list the top health-boosting foods—try to include them in your diet on a regular basis to reap the health benefits associated with eating them.

Fruits and vegetables

Numerous research studies have linked diets that are high in fruits and vegetables with less heart disease, cancer, high blood pressure, and diabetes. Eat *at least* five portions (about 4½ cups/1 pound) per day, preferably more, of fruits and vegetables (excluding potatoes), especially the colorful fruits and vegetables because these are particularly rich in antioxidants and anticancer flavonoids and also carotenoids. Research has shown that people who consume plenty of dark green, yellow, bright orange, deep red, and purple produce have a significantly decreased risk of various cancers.

Fruits and vegetables— top health boosters

açaí berries • alfalfa sprouts • apricots • asparagus • avocados • bananas • beets • berries • broccoli • brussels sprouts • butternut squash • cauliflower • cherries • chilies • corn on the cob • dates • eggplants • fennel • figs • fresh herbs • garlic • ginger • globe artichokes • grapes • green beans • guavas • kale • kiwifruit • mangoes • mushrooms • okra • olives • oranges • papayas • peas • bell peppers • pineapples • plums • pomegranates • potatoes • pumpkins • radishes • raisins • rhubarb • rutabaga • seaweed • snow peas • spinach • sweet potatoes • tomatoes • watercress • watermelons • yams

The high content of fiber in fruits and vegetables also has a big role in maintaining good health. A low-fiber diet causes constipation and over a period of time the bowel can lose its natural strength and elasticity. If there is too little fiber in the diet, the transit time of food residue is slowed, resulting in possible damage, such as diverticulosis—the formation of small pockets in the lining of the gut. Too little fiber may also be a factor in the development of some forms of cancer. In addition, fiber helps to keep levels of blood cholesterol down and helps keep blood sugar levels steady.

Fish, meat, and poultry

Everyone should eat at least two portions of fish per week to boost health, one of which should be oily. Fish is an excellent source of protein, vitamins, and minerals, and it is low in saturated fat. Oily fish (anchovies, herring, mackerel, salmon, sardines, tuna, and whitebait/smelt) is particularly good because of its omega-3 fats, which are believed to help protect against heart disease, arthritis, breast cancer, and dementia. (Because of the potential health risks from the levels of mercury in oily fish, women who are pregnant, breast-feeding or likely to have children in the future should eat no more

Fish, meat, and poultry— top health boosters

anchovies • chicken • cod • game • guinea fowl • herrings • lean red meat • liver • mackerel • mussels • oysters • partridge • pheasant • shrimp • salmon • sardines • scallops • snapper • tuna • turkey • venison • whitebait (smelt)

Grains and legumes—top health boosters

aduki beans • barley • black beans • borlotti beans • brown rice • buckwheat • butter beans • chickpeas • flageolet beans • kidney beans • lentils • millet • haricot beans • oats • pinto beans • quinoa • rye • soy beans • spelt • wheat germ • wheatgrass and wheatgrass juice • whole-grain bread • whole-wheat pasta

than two portions per week; everyone else can eat up to four.)

Research suggests an association between red meat consumption and heart attack, stroke, and bowel cancer. Certainly, you should only eat lean red meat, and avoid meat products such as sausages, hamburgers, luncheon meat, and salami.

Grains and legumes

People whose diets are rich in whole grains and legumes tend to experience less stroke, heart disease, diabetes, and cancer. Whole grains and legumes lower cholesterol levels, which helps keep the heart healthy. They also maintain the health of the digestive and immune systems. By boosting fiber intake, whole grains and legumes promote regular bowel movements, which can help control some types of irritable bowel syndrome, avoid hemorrhoids, and keep the intestines free of diseases, such as diverticular disease and bowel cancer.

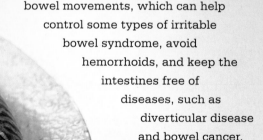

Whole grains in the diet also improve blood sugar control, which helps prevent diabetes. In addition, they are rich in vitamin E, selenium, and lignans, a type of phytoestrogen, all of which are associated with reduced risk of cancer. Compared with people who don't include whole grains in their diet, those who eat whole-grain bread and pasta have been shown by a number of different scientific studies to have a 33 percent lower risk of cancer and heart disease. Try to eat two to three portions of whole grains every day.

Nuts and seeds

Regular consumers of nuts have been shown to have less risk of heart disease and diabetes than those who don't eat nuts.

Seeds contain all the essential nutrients for the growth of healthy new plants and are, therefore, often referred to as little

Nuts and seeds—top health boosters

almonds • brazil nuts • cashews • hazelnuts • peanuts • pine nuts • walnuts • flaxseed (linseed) • poppy seeds • pumpkin seeds • sesame seeds • sunflower seeds

Other top health boosters

Dark chocolate Raw cacao beans are rich in antioxidant flavonoids, so dark chocolate with the minimum of added milk and sugar may be considered a health booster for its antioxidant powers. Cacao beans also contain high levels of some "feel-good" neurotransmitters (serotonin, phenylethylamine, and dopamine). Use real chocolate chips (crushed cacao beans) in cooking to benefit from this health-boosting food.
Spirulina A blue-green algae, spirulina is packed with natural goodness. It has antibacterial and antifungal properties and is good for antiaging. Use it in smoothies in its powdered form.

Other health-boosting foods include: reduced-fat **milk**, low-fat **live yogurt** and **cheese,** and **tofu,** all of which are high-calcium foods and, therefore, help prevent osteoporosis; **eggs, honey,** and **molasses, olive oil** and **tea.**

"powerhouses of nutrition." Try eating them as a snack or adding them to breakfast cereals, salads, and stir-fries, or to bread, cookie, and cake mixtures to boost energy levels and protect yourself against high cholesterol, anemia, osteoporosis, and heart disease.

nutrients & phytonutrients

Opinion is divided as to whether dietary supplements are necessary if you enjoy a balanced diet and eat a wide variety of health-boosting foods. Taking a daily multivitamin and mineral supplement may be a wise insurance policy for good health and certainly won't do you any harm. Bear in mind, however, that even the best one can't possibly replicate all the hundreds of vitamins, minerals, and phytonutrients found in real foods.

Anthocyanidins Berries, cherries, red grapes

Beta-carotene Leafy green vegetables, carrots, pumpkin, butternut squash, apricots, canteloupe melons, mangoes

Biotin Chicken liver, kidney, meat, milk, eggs, beans, whole grains, peanuts, almonds, sesame seeds

Calcium Tinned sardines, milk, cheese, yogurt, oats, beans, lentils, soy, tofu, beets, seaweed, spinach, kale, figs, almonds, cashews, walnuts, pumpkin and sesame seeds

Chromium Beef, chicken, shellfish, eggs, brown rice, whole-grain bread, brewer's yeast, peppers, nuts

Copper Fish, shrimp, lamb's liver, tofu, seaweed, green vegetables, peanuts, cashew nuts

Folate (folic acid) Calf's liver, beans, lentils, fortified breakfast cereals, parsley, leafy green vegetables, spinach, romaine lettuce, watercress, broccoli, brussels sprouts, beets, asparagus, sweet potatoes, peanuts, sesame seeds

Fluoride Fish, tea

Iodine Fish, seafood, milk, eggs, seaweed, watercress, pears

Iron Red meat, liver, eggs, beans, lentils, soy, beets, broccoli, seaweed, sweet potatoes, watercress, mangoes, papayas, pumpkin and sesame seeds

Isoflavones Soy beans and soy products

Lignans Rye, flaxseed (linseed)

Lycopene Tomatoes and processed tomato products, watermelon, guavas, pink grapefruit, rose hip

Manganese Egg yolks, beans, lentils, whole-grain bread, leafy green vegetables, okra, beets, tea, pineapple, blackberries, hazelnuts

Magnesium Shrimp, whole grains, beans, lentils, peas, soy, leafy green vegetables, bell peppers, sweet potatoes, beets, okra, pears, apples, berries, nuts, almonds, cashews, pumpkin and sesame seeds

Omega-3 essential fatty acids Oily fish, flaxseed (linseed), walnuts, mustard seeds

Omega-6 essential fatty acids Nuts and seeds

Phosphorus Fish, shrimp, mussels, meat, turkey, dairy foods, eggs, sweet potatoes, apples, pears

Potassium Chicken, baked potatoes, bananas, prunes, dried apricots, almonds, peanuts

Selenium Shrimp, salmon, snapper, meat, calf's liver, cheese, eggs, cereals, beans, lentils, soy, mushrooms, brazil nuts, walnuts, sesame seeds

Silicon Seaweed

Sodium Most raw foods contain small amounts of sodium chloride (salt) and it is widely found in processed foods such as potato chips, bacon. We all consume too much salt and should halve our intake for the sake of our blood pressure

Sulforaphane Cabbage, cauliflower, broccoli, kale, horseradish

Vitamin A (retinol) Oily fish, organ meat, whole milk, butter, cheese, eggs, beets, broccoli, cabbage, carrots, peppers, spinach, sweet potatoes, tomatoes, watercress, apples, pears, papayas, bananas, berries, cashews, chestnuts, hazelnuts, sunflower seeds

Vitamin B$_1$ (thiamin) Cod's roe (taramasalata), game, wheat germ, whole-grain bread, oatmeal, soya, peas, brazil nuts, peanuts

Vitamin B$_2$ (riboflavin) Game, milk, yogurt, cheese, eggs, wheat germ, broccoli, almonds

Vitamin B$_3$ (niacin) Lamb's liver, tuna, salmon, sardines, halibut, venison, chicken, boiled eggs, whole-grain bread, soya, mushrooms, asparagus, peanuts

Vitamin B$_5$ (pantothenic acid) Fish, meat (especially organ meat), egg yolks, beans, tofu, brewer's yeast, avocados, broccoli, peanuts

Vitamin B$_6$ (pyridoxine) Fish, meat, eggs, whole grains, soy, bell peppers, spinach, beets, bananas, hazelnuts

Vitamin B$_{12}$ (cobalamins) Snapper, flounder, liver, milk, cheese, eggs, yeast extract, fortified breakfast cereals

Vitamin C (ascorbic acid) Potatoes, cauliflower, broccoli, kale, brussels sprouts, bell peppers, chilies, parsley, tomatoes, black currants, strawberries, oranges, lemon juice, papayas, mangoes, guavas, kiwifruits, brazil nuts, chestnuts, hazelnuts

Vitamin D (calciferol) Oily fish, cod liver oil, milk, butter, cheese, egg yolks, fotified margarine, fortified breakfast cereals, sunflower seeds

Vitamin E (tocopherol) Wheat germ and wheat germ oil, olive oil, soy oil, raw and dry-roasted nuts, sunflower and sesame seeds

Vitamin K Fish liver oil, liver, beans, peas, soy oil, margarine, potatoes, carrots, broccoli, brussels sprouts, spinach, leafy green vegetables, sunflower seeds

Zinc Sardines, oysters, crab, beef, lamb, calf's liver, game, cheese, eggs, soy, tofu, seaweed, tomatoes, hazelnuts, pine nuts, pumpkin and sesame seeds

preserving nutrients

Overreliance on processed convenience foods and drinks, with all their chemical additives, extra salt, fat, and sugar, is undoubtedly a contributory factor to ill health in many Western societies today. Many of us are unfit and overweight and, as our bodies struggle to cope with the overload of toxins, we are more likely to succumb to infection and diseases. According to the World Health Organization, dietary factors account for about 30 percent of all cancers in the West.

Processed food

Processing food takes it a long way from its original state as a fresh whole ingredient packed with natural nutrients. For example, polishing whole grain rice to make white rice loses the energizing B vitamins. Generally, the more a food is processed, the less nutrients remain. The exception to this is the lycopene in tomatoes. Because lycopene is fat soluble and tightly bound to fiber, crushing and/or cooking tomatoes makes the lycopene in products, such as canned tomatoes, tomato paste, ketchup, tomato juice, spaghetti sauce, and pizza, more easily absorbed by our bodies than that from raw tomatoes.

Healthy cooking and preparing

Cooking also destroys some nutrients, which is why some people advocate a diet of totally raw whole foods and juices. Certainly, overcooking foods—for too long or at too high a temperature—can destroy many of their beneficial vitamins, minerals, and phytonutrients, and may produce harmful free radicals (see page 24).

As a general rule, cook fruits and vegetables for as short a time as possible—steaming, microwaving, or stir-frying are all good options if cooking is necessary. When boiling vegetables, add them to water that is already rapidly boiling to shorten the cooking time, and don't salt the water because this draws nutrients such as folate, potassium, and vitamin C out of the vegetables and it is lost in the water—unless you use the cooking water for making stock, sauces, or gravy.

Avoid peeling fruits and vegetables so that you retain the minerals and vitamins that are frequently located just beneath the surface of the skin. To minimize nutrient loss, prepare them only just before cooking to delay exposure to the air (oxidation), and never soak them in water.

Shopping wisely

All foods lose nutrients over time, so shopping little and often ensures you always have fresh ingredients at hand—the fresher the food, the more nutrients it contains.

Instead of buying processed already prepared meals, to avoid cooking, choose natural convenience foods that cook speedily or require no cooking at all. You can quickly create delicious meals using vegetables to make salads; whole-grain breads such as pitta; quick-cooking grains such as couscous; pesto for instant pasta sauces; fresh herbs; tinned fish; broiled or griddled fresh meat or fish, such as tuna, salmon, or turkey steaks; baby new potatoes and steamed or microwaved fresh vegetables.

Buy only seasonal produce

Buying produce local to your area and in season ensures that it is fresh, and, therefore, more nutritious than something picked while under ripe, transported from the other side of the world, and ripened artificially in transit. In addition, seasonal produce is inevitably cheaper than imported foods.

Buy organic

Organic produce may be misshapen and covered with mud, but it often has more flavor than conventionally produced items, where the emphasis is on appearance and long shelf life, often at the expense of nutrients. In addition, organic produce and organically farmed meat and poultry won't have come into contact with chemicals that require your body to work harder to expel the toxins.

Correct storage

Storing food correctly is essential for preserving nutrients for as long as possible. Many ingredients, especially once cut open/started, need refrigerating to minimize further nutrient loss. Appropriate storage advice has been supplied for most of the 100 health-boosting foods in this book.

health conditions and complaints—what to eat

Including specific health-boosting foods regularly in your diet may help prevent or reduce the severity of the various conditions and diseases listed below. Use this information as a beginning point, and consult your doctor for detailed medical and nutritional advice.

Anemia

Eating iron-rich foods can help combat anemia. Accompanying them with a vitamin C-rich food/drink will aid the body's absorption of the iron.

Eat more shellfish, red meat, organ meat, chicken, lentils, peas, green beans, dark green leafy vegetables (spinach, kale, watercress), dates, nuts

Drink less tea and coffee with meals because they inhibit iron absorption

Atherosclerosis

Atherosclerosis, a buildup of fatty deposits on artery walls, is a risk factor for heart disease, heart attack, and stroke.

Eat more oily fish, whole grains (especially oats), beans, lentils, soy, alliums (garlic, onions), tomatoes, olive oil, tea, cranberries, grapefruit, kiwifruits, nuts (walnuts, almonds), seeds (sesame, pumpkin, sunflower)

Eat less saturated fats

Cellulite

Your diet can make a difference to the amount of cellulite you have.

Eat more beans, lentils, fibrous vegetables, apples, and seeds to help eliminate waste and toxins and drink more water

Eat less refined and high-fat foods, salt, sugar, coffee, and drink less tea and alcohol

Colds

You can't cure colds through diet, but you can boost your immunity and alleviate the symptoms of a cold.

Eat more vitamin C-rich foods (citrus fruits, berries, kiwifruits, green leafy vegetables), antibacterial foods (onions, garlic), and foods containing zinc (chickpeas, spinach, pumpkin seeds) to shorten the duration of colds

Eat less caffeine, dairy products (opinion is divided as to whether dairy foods encourage the production of mucus)

Constipation

Constipation is caused by a lack of fiber in the diet and is a risk factor for hemorrhoids, diverticulitis, and bowel cancer. Make any dietary changes gradually to allow your digestive system to adapt.

Eat more insoluble fiber-rich foods (whole grains, brown rice, whole-grain bread) and foods high in soluble fiber (oats, beans, green leafy vegetables, apples, pears, apricots, figs, prunes), plus plenty of water

Eat less refined and processed foods

Depression

Focus on foods that boost your levels of the "happy" brain chemical serotonin.

Eat more foods containing tryptophan (bread, potatoes, cauliflowers, bananas, dates, hazelnuts) and B vitamins (meat, organ meat, chicken, whole grains, wheat germ, legumes, most vegetables, yeast, nuts, and seeds)

Drink less alcohol and caffeinated drinks

Exhaustion and fatigue

A better diet will keep you energized throughout the day.

Eat more oily fish, onions, garlic, nuts and seeds, low-glycaemic index carbohydrates (such as slow-release energy foods such as oats), iron-rich foods (lean red meat, liver, spinach, apricots) and drink more water

Eat less: caffeine, saturated and trans fats, and high-glycaemic index carbohydrate foods, such as cakes, pastries, soft drinks

Gout

You may be able to control gout (an excess of uric acid in the blood) with diet instead of medication.

Eat more lentils, green leafy vegetables, watercress, celery, beets, grapefruit, pineapple, cherries

Eat less protein-rich foods (fish, shellfish, red meat, organ meat, oats, mushrooms); fried foods and refined carbohydrates; sweet fruits (such as grapes); sugar; drink less alcohol and coffee

Hangover

Speedy recovery involves drinking plenty of fluids and eliminating toxins from your system.

Eat more globe artichokes (to restore the liver); onions, garlic, green vegetables, apples, pears, and citrus fruit (to help the body detoxify); low-glycaemic index food, such as oats (to control your blood sugar levels). Drink more water and vitamin C-rich fruit juices (to rehydrate you)

Eat less saturated fats, processed foods; drink less coffee

High blood pressure (hypertension)

It is essential to reduce high blood pressure because it is a risk factor for stroke, heart disease, and kidney disease.

Eat more: oily fish, high-fiber foods (oats, whole grains, beans), soy, olive oil, alliums (garlic, onions, leeks, chives, scallions), green leafy vegetables, broccoli, potatoes, beans, celery, avocadoes, apples, citrus fruit, nuts (brazil nuts, almonds, walnuts), seeds (flaxseed, sunflower seeds, pine nuts, sesame seeds) **Eat less** salt, caffeine, refined carbohydrate foods (cakes, pastries), saturated fats, meat products (bacon, sausages, pâté, meat pies); drink less alcohol

High cholesterol

Left unchecked, high blood cholesterol levels can cause arterial disease, such as atherosclerosis (narrowing of the arteries), heart attacks, and strokes.

Eat more oily fish, high-fiber foods (whole grains, oats, bran, barley, brown rice, beans, peas), olive oil, vitamin C-rich foods (kiwifruits, citrus fruit, peppers, broccoli), vitamin E-rich foods (almonds, walnuts), seeds (sesame, pumpkin, sunflower)

Eat less saturated fats and processed foods

Insomnia

Tryptophan, a relaxing substance connected with the production of serotonin, is present in some foods and appears to encourage sleep.

Eat more tryptophan-releasing foods (chicken, turkey, pasta, rice, beans, potatoes, root vegetables, basil, lettuce, broccoli, figs, dates, bananas, hazelnuts)

Eat less high-protein foods and drink less caffeine in the evening

Irritable bowel syndrome (IBS)

Certain foods trigger the symptoms of IBS in some people. Learn your triggers and avoid them. It may also help to avoid large meals.

If constipation is a symptom of your IBS:

Eat more high-fiber foods (whole grains, oats, bran, broccoli, cabbage, beans, peas, fruits), add these to your diet gradually to avoid worsening gas or cramps; drink more water

If diarrhea is a symptom of your IBS:

Eat more startchy foods (whole-wheat bread and pasta, brown rice, live yogurt

For both symptoms:

Eat less fatty and spicy foods and milk products, and drink less alcohol and caffeine

Low male fertility

Bear in mind that being overweight can also affect fertility.

Eat more vitamin C-rich foods, beta-carotene foods (orange and dark green fruits and vegetables), zinc-rich foods (such as shellfish, pumpkin seeds)

Drink less alcohol and caffeinated drinks

Menopausal problems

Eating phytoestrogen-containing foods can help correct the hormonal imbalance, also though their estrogen-like effect is weak compared to the strength of the naturally occurring estrogens in a woman's body.

Eat more oily fish, whole grains, brown rice, beans, lentils, chickpeas, soy beans and soy products, alfalfa, peas, beets, fennel, broccoli, celery, seeds
Eat less sugar, saturated fats; drink less coffee

Osteoarthritis

Osteo- and rheumatoid arthirtis are the two most common types of arthritis. Certain foods help halt the progression of this joint disease and deal with the pain and inflammation.
Eat more oily fish, whole grains, beans, fresh fruits and vegetables, sweet potatoes, ginger, walnuts, chestnuts, flaxseed
Eat less highly refined products, saturated and trans fats; drink fewer carbonated drinks

Osteoporosis

Eating bone-strengthening foods throughout your life can help prevent osteoporosis in later life or mitigate the resulting damage.
Eat more seafood, calcium- and vitamin D-rich foods (low-fat dairy products or fortified soy products), olive oil, beans, peas, green leafy vegetables, apples, flaxseed
Eat less refined sugar, salt, saturated fat. Drink less coffee, alcohol, fewer carbonated drinks

Premenstrual syndrome (PMS)

Cut down on refined and processed foods and eat as much freshly prepared food as possible.
Eat more oily fish, shellfish, whole grains, oats, brown rice, soy products, beans, lentils, chickpeas, bean sprouts, peas, beets, fennel, sweet potatoes, broccoli, brussels sprouts, rhubarb, flaxseed, sunflower seeds and pumpkin seeds
Eat less spicy foods, chocolate, cakes, cookies, drink less coffee, alcohol

Prostate gland problems

Eating foods high in phytoestrogens may be beneficial for prostate problems.
Eat more oily fish, shellfish, eggs, soy beans and soy products, chickpeas, lentils, peas, fennel, tomatoes and tomato products, avocados, molasses, nuts, flaxseed; drink more green tea, red wine
Eat less processed foods

Rheumatoid arthritis

Improving diet may help reduce the pain and prevent some of the disability associated with this form of arthritis.
Eat more white and oily fish, eggs, olive oil, fresh fruits and vegetables, sunflower seeds
Eat less saturated fat, dairy foods, omega-6 fatty acids (polyunsaturated oils)

Stress

Diet can play a part in tackling stress (a risk factor for heart disease).
Eat more oily fish, skinless chicken, low-fat dairy products, unrefined whole foods (whole-grain bread, pasta, rice, oats), fruits
Eat less red meat, "junk food," sugary foods, take-out foods; drink less caffeine, alcohol.

the 100 foods

apples

Apples were introduced to the West by the Romans, and today there are more than 2,000 different cultivars. An apple a day really does help keep the doctor away, thanks to apples' potent **antioxidant phytochemicals,** which help protect the heart, contribute to a healthy urinary tract, and healthy vision, and bolster **anticancer** defenses.

The soluble fiber in apples, pectin, **helps lower blood cholesterol** levels, reducing the risk of heart disease. Pectin also improves the efficiency of the digestive system by removing toxic metals, such as lead and mercury from the body. Apples are, therefore, good for a detoxification program and especially useful if you live in traffic-heavy urban areas.

Ideal as a low-calorie snack, apples release sugar slowly into the bloodstream and are great for helping raise flagging energy levels.

✱ **storing and serving** Buy organic fruit whenever possible to avoid residual pesticides, and wash thoroughly. Eat unpeeled or juiced whole, including the pips, for maximum nutritional benefit. The fresher the apple, the more vitamin C it contains.

baked apples with lemon

1 Core **4 large eating apples** and enlarge the holes with a small knife. Score around the middle of each apple so the skins do not burst.

2 Cut **1 lemon** lengthways into 4. Roll the lemon pieces in a mixture of ¼ **cup light brown sugar** and **1 teaspoon ground cinnamon.** Push a coated lemon wedge into each apple cavity.

3 Bake the apples in a foil-lined dish in a preheated oven set to 350°F for 45 minutes. Serve with fromage frais or yogurt. **serves 4**

NUTRITIONAL CONTENT PER APPLE (SMALL): energy 47 calories | **protein** 0.4 g | **carbohydrates** 12 g | **fat** 0 g | **fiber** 2 g | **vitamin C** 6 mg | **potassium** 120 mg | **calcium** 4 mg

41

pears

Like apples, pears provide plenty of fiber, including the soluble fiber pectin, which helps cleanse the colon and keep it healthy, and to **lower blood cholesterol** levels, which helps protect the heart. Also, like apples, pears help rid the body of toxins, and a detoxification program of pears alone for a day or so will deep cleanse your digestive system and benefit your skin.

Although not especially rich in nutrients, pears contain vitamins A, C, E, and K and some **potassium** and copper, and their **iodine** can aid thyroid function. The protective antioxidants in pears include the flavonoid epicatechin, which helps fight the free radicals linked to the negative effects of aging.

Canned pears are nutritionally inferior to fresh ones, containing not only between a half and two-thirds less vitamin C and fiber, but also more calories.

✷ **storing and serving** Ripe pears do not keep well and bruise easily, so choose firm, unwrinkled fruit, preferably organic to avoid pesticide residues. Store them out of direct sunlight or in the refrigerator if they are already ripe. Eat fresh pears, with the skin, as soon as possible for maximum nutritional benefit.

pear and stilton salad

1 Core and quarter **4 pears** and slice each quarter in half. Cook the pear slices on a preheated griddle pan for 1 minute on each side. Transfer to a plate and sprinkle over **4 tablespoons lemon juice**.

2 Arrange **5-6 cups baby spinach** (or mixed lettuce leaves) on 4 plates, arrange the griddled pears on top, and sprinkle with **4 chopped walnuts, 2 cups crumbled Stilton cheese,** and **4 tablespoons walnut oil**. Serve immediately. **serves 4**

NUTRITIONAL CONTENT PER PEAR (LARGE): energy 80 calories I **protein** 0.3 g I **carbohydrates** 20 g I **fat** 0.2 g I **fiber** 4 g I **vitamin C** 12 mg I **potassium** 150 mg I **calcium** 22 mg

bananas

The high **potassium** levels in bananas means that eating them regularly can help **maintain a healthy heart, control blood pressure,** and **promote healthy bones.** Bananas are also full of the vital antioxidants beta-carotene (the precursor to vitamin A) and vitamin C, both of which **boost the immune system** and protect against heart disease and some cancers.

The vitamin B_6 in bananas regulates the nervous system and helps promote healthy skin, while the amino acid tryptophan may help reduce symptoms of premenstrual syndrome (PMS), anxiety, and insomnia.

Their high fiber content makes bananas mildly laxative, but ripe ones can help alleviate diarrhea. A source of slow-release energy, they are great for breakfast or as a snack, and they can be eaten before, during, or after exercise. Dried bananas also make a good snack, with higher levels of fiber and potassium.

✽ storing and serving Choose firm yellow bananas and store them at room temperature away from other fruits to avoid becoming over-ripe. Although they look unappealing, browny-black bananas are ideal weaning food for babies.

banana and peanut butter smoothie

1 Peel and slice **1 ripe banana** and freeze it for at least 2 hours or overnight.

2 Put the frozen banana in a blender or food processor with **1¼ cups semi-skimmed milk** and **1 tablespoon smooth peanut butter (or 2 teaspoons tahini paste)** and process until smooth.

3 Pour into a glass and serve immediately. **serves 1**

NUTRITIONAL CONTENT PER BANANA (MEDIUM, NO SKIN): energy 95 calories | **protein** 1.2 g | **carbohydrates** 23 g | **fat** 0.3 g | **fiber** 3 g | **vitamin C** 11 mg | **potassium** 400 mg

45

NUTRITIONAL CONTENT PER 20 GRAPES: energy 60 calories I protein 0.4 g I carbohydrates 15 g I fat 0.1 g I fiber 1 g I vitamin C 3 mg I potassium 210 mg I magnesium 7 mg

grapes

Red (black) grapes and red wine have long been recognized as providing some protection against heart disease and red or purple grape juice is believed to offer the same health benefits. This is attributed to the health-boosting compounds in grapes, particularly the flavonoids quercitin and resveratrol. Resveratrol, found in red grape skins, has strong **antioxidant** and **anti-inflammatory** properties and is believed to help prevent cancer, to improve blood flow to the brain, thus reducing the risk of stroke, and to make the blood less likely to clot.

Green (white) grapes contain little or no resveratrol, but the high quantity of other antioxidants in both types of grapes is believed to lower cholesterol levels, reduce the risk of cancer, and boost brain power.

Raisins are grapes that have been dehydrated and are an equally rich source of antioxidants.

✱ **storing and serving** Store grapes, unwashed, in the refrigerator, and keep them on their stems until required. Just before use, wash well under running water to remove pesticide residues, but don't peel or you will remove many of the important nutrients. Eat as a snack, serve with cheese, or use in salads.

black grape jelly with citrus fruits

1 Gently heat ⅔ **cup red grape juice** with **package gelatin.** Let cool. Mix the dissolved gelatine with **2 cups red grape juice**.

2 Put **1 cup halved red and green grapes** in 4 glasses; pour over the jello. Chill until set.

3 Segment **1 orange** and **1 pink grapefruit,** collecting the juice in a pan. Add **1 tablespoon sugar** and heat until dissolved. Bring to a simmer, then add the segments and let cool.

4 To serve, spoon the citrus segments and a little juice on the jello. **serves 4**

47

grapefruit

Grapefruit help promote a healthy heart, being a rich source of vitamin C and bioflavonoids, which protect the arteries and improve blood circulation. **Folic acid** and **potassium** further help protect the heart.

Grapefruit also have **anticancer** properties. Pink and red types have a significant quantity of **lycopene,** believed to reduce the risk of prostate cancer. They also contain a number of other cancer-inhibiting compounds, including **limonene,** found in all citrus oils, that may help reduce tumor growth.

The bitter-tasting flavonoid compound **naringin,** thought to inhibit the uptake of fatty acids into cells, thus preventing the body from using carbohydrates effectively, makes grapefruit good for weight loss.

Grapefruit pectin, the soluble fiber found in the white pith between segments, is good for **lowering blood cholesterol levels** and detoxifying.

✱ **storing and serving** Grapefruit can be left in the fruit bowl for a week or in the refrigerator for several weeks. Bring to room temperature before use because the fruit is at its juiciest when slightly warm.

pink grapefruit and pine nut salad

1 Peel and segment **2 pink grapefruits,** working over a dish to collect the juice.

2 Halve, stone and peel **2 avocados.** Slice the flesh and mix with the reserved citrus juice.

3 Lightly toast ⅔ **cup pine nuts** under a broiler, or dry-fry them in a frying pan. Sprinkle the nuts over the avocado and grapefruit and offer grated **Parmesan cheese** separately. **serves 4**

NUTRITIONAL CONTENT PER GRAPEFRUIT (MEDIUM): energy 105 calories I **protein** 4 g I **carbohydrates** 25 g I **fat** 0 g I **fiber** 10 g I **vitamin C** 126 mg I **potassium** 700 mg I **calcium** 8 mg

lemons and limes

The health-boosting powers of lemons and limes have long been known. In the eighteenth century, British sailors were given a ration of lime juice every day to prevent scurvy (a deficiency disease caused by lack of vitamin C); this earned them their nickname "limeys."

Like all citrus fruit, lemons and limes contain loads of **Vitamin C,** which helps white blood cells fight infection, boosts immunity in general, and helps maintain mental alertness and a retentive memory. It is also needed for healing wounds and may help reduce some of the symptoms of arthritis.

Other antioxidants in citrus fruit, bioflavonoids, work with vitamin C to strengthen blood vessel walls, reducing the risk of stroke and heart disease. Studies suggest that the citrus oil **limonene** can reduce the growth of cancerous tumors and possibly **lower blood cholesterol.**

✱ **storing and serving** Lemons will keep for a week or two at room temperature and for longer if refrigerated. Limes are best kept in the refrigerator. You will get the most juice from the fruit if you let it stand at room temperature and roll it on a flat surface before squeezing.

lemon and basil penne

1 Cook **1½ cups dried penne** in boiling water according to the instructions on the package.

2 Meanwhile, blend together **2 garlic cloves,** a large **handful of basil leaves, 4 tablespoons olive oil,** and the grated rind and juice of **2 lemons.** Add ½ **cup grated Parmesan** and season with **pepper** to taste.

3 Drain the pasta, stir through the pesto, and serve immediately. **serves 4**

oranges

Oranges are known for their high vitamin C content, which is important for a **healthy immune system** and helps the body disarm the cell-damaging free radicals that accelerate aging and cause diseases such as cancer, heart disease and strokes.

Oranges are packed with plenty of other health boosters, including fiber, which helps **keep cholesterol levels down** and the digestive system operating efficiently, and powerful **flavonoids,** such as herperidin, which is even more effective than vitamin C in fighting high cholesterol levels, high blood pressure, and other factors implicated in diseases.

Research has linked a citrus-rich diet with a reduced risk of certain cancers. This is due to a compound found in citrus oils called **limonene,** which is believed to reduce the growth of tumors.

✳ storing and serving Oranges can be stored at room temperature or in the refrigerator. Most of the potent phytonutrients are found in the peel (and the oil it contains), so use the rind whenever possible in baking and desserts. However, avoid using fruit that has been waxed to improve its appearance.

carrot soup with orange and ginger

1 Peel and roughly chop **7–10 pounds carrots** and finely chop a **2 inch piece of fresh ginger root.** Add to a saucepan containing **3¾ cups vegetable stock (or water).** Bring to a boil, then simmer for 12–15 minutes, or until cooked through.

2 Stir **2 tablespoons chopped parsley** into the soup and process in batches with **⅔ cup orange juice.** Season to taste with **salt and pepper.**

3 Return to the pan, simmer gently to reheat, and serve with a little **buttermilk (or plain yogurt)** swirled on top. **serves 6**

NUTRITIONAL CONTENT PER 100G ORANGE (PEELED): energy 34 calories | **protein** 1.1 g | **carbohydrates** 9 g | **fat** 0.1 g | **fiber** 2 g | **vitamin C** 54 mg | **potassium** 150 mg | **calcium** 47 mg

53

NUTRITIONAL CONTENT PER 100 G: energy 36 calories I **protein** 0.5 g I **carbohydrates** 9 g I **fat** 0 g I **fiber** 2 g I **vitamin C** 60 mg I **potassium** 200 mg I **calcium** 23 mg I **magnesium** 11 mg

papayas

Containing more vitamin C and **potassium** than oranges, papayas are **nutritional super foods.** They are packed with cholesterol-lowering fiber and with antioxidants, including the eye-saving carotenoids lutein and zeaxanthin; lycopene, which is linked with prostate health; and the phytochemicals carpaine and cryptoxanthin, which are believed to help protect from cancer.

The high levels of beta-carotene (which the body converts to vitamin A) and vitamin C work together, making this tropical fruit great for the **immune system.** They also help maintain healthy skin by encouraging elasticity, hindering the formation of wrinkles, and keeping skin cells plump.

Papayas are great for detoxifying the body. They contain papain, a digestive enzyme that helps break down protein and cleanse the digestive tract, which can, in turn, help with weight loss.

✳ **storing and serving** Papayas are best when ripe. They should have a strong fragrance, and the skin should be firm but yield to pressure. Leave them in the fruit bowl to ripen, then store in the refrigerator and eat within a day or two. Halve lengthways, scoop out the seeds, and eat the flesh with a spoon.

broiled fruit

1 Halve **1 large papaya,** remove the seeds, then peel and slice the flesh. Peel and slice the flesh from **1 large mango.** Peel and cut **2 bananas** in half and slice the pieces in half lengthways. Peel and thinly slice **2 oranges.**

2 Arrange the fruits in a foil-lined broiler pan and dot with **2 tablespoons unsalted butter.** Sprinkle with **3 tablespoons brown sugar** and cook under a hot broiler for 10–15 minutes, turning occasionally and basting with the melted sugar, butter, and fruit juices. Serve with **plain yogurt. serves 4**

figs

Figs are good for the digestive system. They are packed with fiber and also contain ficin, an enzyme that helps soothe the gut. They are mildly laxative.

Figs contain compounds that help shrink tumors and are, therefore, believed to help prevent cancer. They are also one of the highest plant sources of **calcium,** which is required for good bone health, blood clotting, and healthy nerve function.

The other nutrients in figs, including **iron** and **potassium,** are particularly concentrated in dried figs, which provide instant energy and help prevent cramps, so making them ideal for athletes. The amino acid tryptophan makes figs a natural sedative.

Figs appear to trigger headaches in some people. The oxalates in them make them unsuitable for people suffering from kidney or gallbladder problems.

✱ **storing and serving** Keep under-ripe figs at room temperature out of direct sunlight. Store ripe figs in the refrigerator but bring to room temperature to serve. Use fresh figs raw as a snack, serve them in salads or with cheese, or poach them for desserts. Use dried figs in breakfast cereals and baking.

fig, mozzarella, and parma ham salad

1 Cut **8 ripe black figs** into quarters and tear **2 cups mozzarella** and **8 slices parma ham** or **prosciutto** into bite-size pieces. Arrange them all on a large platter with a few **basil leaves.**

2 Whisk together **3 tablespoons olive oil, 1 tablespoon white wine vinegar,** and a **pinch of sugar.**

3 Season the dressing with **salt and pepper** and drizzle over the salad. **serves 4**

NUTRITIONAL CONTENT PER 100 G FRESH (DRIED): **energy** 43 (227) calories I **protein** 1.3 (3.6) g I **carbohydrates** 10 (53) g I **fat** 0.3 (1.6) g I **fiber** 2 (12) g I **vitamin C** 2 (1) mg I **potassium** 200 (970) mg

57

mangoes

Another orange-colored fruit with plenty of beta-carotene (the precursor to vitamin A in the body), the mango is similar to the papaya, with its package of antioxidant and detoxifying phytonutrients.

Mangoes have powerful **immunity-boosting properties,** thanks to the antioxidant vitamins A, C, and E they contain. These roam the body, neutralizing the cell-damaging free radicals responsible for premature aging and degenerative diseases, such as clogged arteries, strokes, heart disease, and cancer.

Packed with soluble fiber, which has cholesterol-removing properties, and insoluble fiber, which helps maintain bowel health, mangoes are also good for the digestive system and useful for soothing indigestion.

The detoxifying properties of mangoes mean they are good for cleansing the kidneys and blood and can help improve skin texture.

✹ **storing and serving** A ripe mango is firm to the touch but with a little "give." Leave under-ripe fruit in the fruit bowl to ripen, then refrigerate. Add mangoes to smoothies for the flavor, although the thick juice is best thinned with apple or pear juice.

mango, avocado, and chicken

1 Halve, stone, and peel **2 ripe avocados.** Dice the flesh and transfer to a shallow bowl with **2 tablespoons lemon juice.**

2 Peel, stone, and dice the flesh of **1 small mango.**

3 Mix **3 tablespoons olive oil, 1 teaspoon whole-grain mustard, 1 teaspoon clear honey, 2 teaspoons cider vinegar,** and **salt and pepper.** Add the lemon juice from the avocado.

4 Arrange **¼ cup sliced cooked beet** and a handful of **watercress** in a bowl and add the avocado and mango. Add the dressing and **6 ounces thinly sliced smoked chicken. serves 4**

NUTRITIONAL CONTENT PER 100 G: energy 57 calories | **protein** 0.7 g | **carbohydrates** 14 g | **fat** 0.2 g | **fiber** 3 g | **vitamin C** 37 mg | **carotene** 1,800 mcg | **potassium** 180 mg | **calcium** 12 mg

59

apricots

Apricots are rich in beta-carotene, which offers some protection against cancer and eye problems, such as cataracts, by neutralizing the free radicals that damage body cells and tissues. Beta-carotene and lycopene, another antioxidant present, also help prevent the formation of plaque in arteries, which can result in high blood pressure and heart disease.

Fresh apricots are rich in vitamin C, and they help regulate the digestive system, because they are especially helpful in relieving constipation. The soluble fiber pectin also helps to **lower blood cholesterol.**

Dried apricots have an increased concentration of beta-carotene, **iron, potassium, calcium,** and magnesium. Iron is needed to form hemoglobin in blood cells, potassium benefits blood pressure, and calcium and magnesium are needed for strong healthy bones and to help prevent osteoporosis.

✱ **choosing dried apricots** Avoid dried apricots preserved with sulfur dioxide because this can trigger asthma attacks. Any pesticide residues are more concentrated in the dried fruit, so choose organic brands, especially for children.

poached apricots with oatmeal cream

1 Heat **2 tablespoons light brown sugar, ½ teaspoon ground ginger,** and **5 tablespoons water** until the sugar has dissolved.

2 Quarter and pit **8–12 medium (1 pound) fresh apricots,** add to the pan, cover, and simmer gently for about 10 minutes. Cool slightly.

3 Meanwhile, dry-fry **½ cup rolled oats** for about 30 seconds. Cool slightly, then stir into **1 cup plain yogurt** and **2 tablespoons heavy cream** and **2 tablespoons honey.** Spoon over the apricots and serve. **serves 4**

NUTRITIONAL CONTENT PER 100 G FRESH (DRIED): energy 29 (158) calories I **protein** 1 (4) g I **carbohydrates** 7 (37) g I **fat** 0 (1) g I **fiber** 2 (18) g I **vitamin** 5 (1) mg I **potassium** 250 (1380) mg

61

NUTRITIONAL CONTENT PER 100 G: energy 49 calories I protein 1.1 g I carbohydrates 11 g I fat 0.5 g I fiber 2 g I **vitamin C** 59 mg I **potassium** 290 mg I **calcium** 25 mg I **magnesium** 15 mg

kiwifruits

Kiwifruits, once known as Chinese gooseberries, are packed with antioxidants, including high levels of vitamins C and E; kiwifruits actually contain more vitamin C than oranges—so eating kiwifruits can help boost immunity and ward off cancer, heart disease, and other degenerative diseases and conditions. They can also help the body deal with stress. Another antioxidant, lutein, helps maintain healthy vision. Kiwifruits also contain **potassium,** needed for healthy blood pressure, and **folate,** important before and during pregnancy to protect against birth defects.

Current research shows that kiwifruits can help with respiratory-related disorders and may provide an alternative to aspirin for thinning the blood to reduce the risk of clots and protect cardiovascular health.

Kiwifruits are also a good source of digestive enzymes, including atinidin, which aid digestion.

✱ **storing and serving** Ripe kiwifruits will keep in the refrigerator for one to two weeks. Store them away from other fruits that emit ethylene gas, which will overripen kiwifruits. To serve, cut the peeled fruit into slices or wedges, or cut the top off the unpeeled fruit like a boiled egg and eat with a spoon.

kiwifruits, melon, and grape salad

1 Cut a thin slice from the base of **1 large Galia melon,** slice off the top, and discard the seeds. Scoop the flesh into small balls. Reserve the shell.

2 Skin ½ **cup seedless green grapes,** thinly slice **3 kiwifruits** and peel, core and thinly slice **2 apples.** Put the fruits in a bowl with the melon balls and a drained **11-ounce can lychees.** Sprinkle with **3 tablespoons kirsch,** cover, and chill until ready to serve.

3 Put the melon shell on a serving plate, pile the fruits into the shell, and decorate with **mint sprigs. serves 4–6**

63

NUTRITIONAL CONTENT PER 100 G FLESH: energy 26 calories | protein 1 g |
carbohydrates 5 g | fat 1 g | fiber 5 g | **vitamin C** 230 mg | carotene 435 mcg | potassium 230 mg

guavas

Guavas are tropical fruit with edible skin and seeds and a pungent fragrance. They are a **top antioxidant fruit,** containing more vitamin C and more lycopene than probably any other known fruit or vegetable, and the red- or pink-fleshed guavas are especially high in lycopene. Guavas are also rich in beta-carotene (the precursor to vitamin A in the body) and soluble fiber. These four nutrients, plus others, including **potassium,** help maintain healthy **blood cholesterol levels** and blood pressure levels and account for guavas' outstanding contribution to heart health.

As well as boosting heart health, lycopene (the same antioxidant carotenoid that gives the red color to tomatoes and watermelon) is also believed to help prevent cancer, particularly prostate cancer.

In addition, guavas are thought to have **antimicrobial** properties and are used in the tropics to treat diarrhea.

✱ **storing and serving** Because vitamin C reduces with each day of storage, look for unblemished fruit when buying and eat as soon as possible after purchase. Eat guavas fresh as long as they are ripe, or use them in jams, fruit salad, and desserts, such as custards and ice cream.

guava, apple, and banana smoothie

1 Peel, halve, and deseed **2 ripe guavas** and roughly chop the flesh. Peel, core, and roughly chop **1 apple** and thickly slice **2 bananas.** Process the fruits together until smooth.

2 Add **1 cup raspberries (or strawberries)** together with **1 cup plain yogurt** and **150 ml (²⁄₃ cup cold water.** Process again until smooth. Pour over ice cubes and drink immediately. **serves 4**

NUTRITIONAL CONTENT PER 100 G FLESH: energy 41 calories | protein 0.4 g | carbohydrates 10 g | fat 0.2 g | fibre 1 g | vitamin C 12 mg | potassium 160 mg | magnesium 16 mg

pineapples

Eating pineapple can aid digestion and help reduce inflammation due to the high levels of the enzyme bromelain. This acts by digesting protein, making it helpful for **clearing a sluggish digestive system,** and by breaking down areas of inflamed body tissue, thus making pineapple useful for sufferers of osteoarthritis, gout, hay fever, and asthma. Eating pineapple on its own between meals maximizes bromelain's **anti-inflammatory** effect. Bromelain also helps prevent blood clots and promotes the healing of minor injuries, and has **anticancer** properties.

Pineapples are rich in beta-carotene and vitamin C, two of the many antioxidants that protect the body from free radicals that cause degenerative diseases.

The vitamin B_1 in pineapple helps energy production, the **potassium** helps regulate blood pressure, while the high manganese content helps protect against hardening of the arteries and is vital for forming bones and cartilage and for maintaining a good **immune system.**

✱ **storing and serving** A pineapple will not ripen once picked, so check your pineapple is ripe—there should be a sweet smell at the stem end. Add fresh pineapple to salads and salsa or griddle for dessert.

baked pineapple rings with cinnamon

1 Peel and core **1 small pineapple** and cut it into ½-inch rings. Pat them dry on paper towel.

2 Combine ¼ **cup brown sugar, 1 teaspoon ground cinnamon,** and a **pinch of mild chili powder** in a plastic bag. Add the pineapple rings and toss well to coat.

3 Arrange the pineapple on a foil-lined baking sheet, dust with **sugar,** and bake in a preheated oven set to 400°F, for 20 minutes. Serve with **fromage frais** or **plain yogurt. serves 4**

67

pomegranates

Recent studies of the health-boosting properties of the **antioxidant-rich** pomegranate suggest that the antioxidant action of its juice is three times more potent than a similar quantity of red wine or green tea, so a daily glass may reduce the risk of heart disease thanks to its tannins, polyphenols, and anthocyanidins, which work by improving the function of blood vessels and reducing hardening of the arteries, as well as **reducing blood cholesterol levels** and high blood pressure. Research suggests that a daily glass is also great for prostate health and may slow the growth of prostate and other tumors, thanks to the high levels of **flavonoids** (antioxidants that are effective at disarming free radicals).

The phytoestrogens (natural estrogen) in pomegranates mean they may also be useful for treating some symptoms of the menopause.

✻ storing and serving Keep pomegranates in the refrigerator for up to three months; at room temperature they will last only two to three days. Use the pulp and seeds in salads and relishes; use the fruit in drinks and sauces.

pomegranate and mixed-leaf salad

1 Put **3 tablespoons raspberry vinegar** and **2 tablespoons olive oil** in a salad bowl, season with **salt and pepper,** and mix lightly.

2 Cut **1 pomegranate** in half, break or cut it into large pieces, and flex the skin so that the seeds fall out. Pick out and discard any stubborn seeds. Add the remainder to the salad bowl, discarding the skin and pith.

3 Toss **4 cups mixed lettuce leaves** (including baby spinach leaves, red mustard, and mizuna) in the dressing, tearing large leaves into bite-sized pieces. Serve sprinkled with **fresh raspberries,** if you want.
serves 6

NUTRITIONAL CONTENT PER 100 G FLESH: energy 72 calories I **protein** 1 g I carbohydrates 17 g I **fat** 1 g I **fiber** 1 g I **vitamin C** 7 mg I **potassium** 379 mg I **magnesium** 12 mg

69

blueberries

Try to eat a handful a day of these antioxidant foods. Blueberries are **packed with anthocyanidins,** which help fight infection and inflammation. They neutralize harmful free radicals and help maintain a healthy vascular system, protecting against varicose veins, heart disease, hemorrhoids, and hardening of the arteries.

Anthocyanidins in blueberries may slow and even **reverse age-related mental decline,** and they can lessen brain damage inflicted by strokes.

Blueberries also contain pterostilbene, which fights cancer, and the soluble fiber pectin, which is thought to help prevent cancer; both compounds help **reduce blood cholesterol** levels. Blueberries also benefit night vision and can help treat diarrhea and constipation.

Unrelated to blueberries but similar in appearance, **açaí berries** are thought to be even higher in antioxidants than blueberries and are one of the most nutritious and powerful foods in the world. They are currently the subject of much research.

✳ storing and serving Blueberries should be eaten fresh or frozen on the day of purchase.

blueberry and raspberry brûlée

1 Arrange a mixture of ¾ **cups blueberries** and ¾ **cups raspberries** in 4 heatproof dishes.

2 Spoon **1½ cups fromage frais** or **plain yogurt** over the fruit and smooth the surface.

3 Sprinkle **4–6 tablespoons soft dark brown sugar** evenly over the top and cook under a preheated hot broiler, for 1–2 minutes, or until the sugar has melted and is bubbling. **serves 4**

NUTRITIONAL CONTENT PER 100 G: energy 57 calories I **protein** 1 g I **carbohydrates** 15 g I **fat** 0.3 g I **fiber** 2 g I **vitamin C** 10 mg I **potassium** 77 mg I **calcium** 6 mg I **magnesium** 6 mg

71

raspberries

All berries are brimming with the vitamins and antioxidants that help protect against premature aging and diseases, such as cancer. In raspberries, the health-boosting antioxidant phytonutrients include **ellagic acid,** which may help prevent the growth of cancerous cells, and a group of flavonoids called anthocyanidins, which have **antimicrobial** properties and can prevent the overgrowth of certain fungi and bacteria in the body, such as the yeast *Candida albicans,* which causes thrush.

Raspberries also help reduce the risk of coronary heart disease. Their fiber content helps lower the levels of "bad" cholesterol in the body, while their antioxidants help decrease the buildup of "bad" cholesterol on artery walls.

Mildy laxative, raspberries are good for indigestion and can help alleviate diarrhea. They are also effective for menstrual and menopausal problems.

✱ storing and serving Raspberries are highly perishable, so store in the refrigerator and use within a day or two. They freeze well—use frozen berries within a year.

raspberry and passionfruit fool

1 Whip together **1 cup evaporated milk** and **1 tablespoon sugar** until the mixture is thick and fluffy.

2 Process **1½ cups raspberries** until smooth, then stir into the whipped evaporated milk with **1½ whole raspberries** and the flesh of **2 passionfruits.** Spoon into serving dishes and serve.
serves 4

NUTRITIONAL CONTENT PER 100 G: energy 25 calories I **protein** 1 g I**carbohydrates** 5 g I **fat** 0 g I **fiber** 7 g I **vitamin C** 32 mg I **potassium** 170 mg I **calcium** 25 mg I **magnesium** 19 mg

73

blackberries

Like raspberries, blackberries contain anthocyanidins, which have strong antioxidant and **anti-inflammatory** properties. Their high tannin content gives them an astringent action, so they can neutralize excessive acid in the body, helping to relieve joint pains. They help sore throats and chesty coughs and help clear diarrhea and urinary tract infections.

Rich in **vitamin E,** blackberries promote a healthy heart and good circulation. They also boost the blood and help prevent anemia. Pectin, the soluble fiber in blackberries, helps **reduce blood cholesterol** levels, thereby reducing the risk of heart disease and stroke.

The aspirin-like compounds in blackberries, salicylates, are thought to lower the risk of heart problems, but if you are intolerant of aspirin you may have an allergic reaction to blackberries.

✱ storing and serving Choose shiny berries with a rich aroma and use them as soon as possible, washing them just before use. Blackberries freeze well; open-freeze on trays, then bag and seal—keep for up to six months.

blackberry and oat layer

1 Spread **1⅓ cup rolled oats** with **2 tablespoons clear honey** on a baking sheet. Cook in a preheated oven set to 350°F, for 10–15 minutes, stirring twice.

2 Remove from the oven, add **2 tablespoons chopped stem ginger,** and let cool. Stir the oats to break up any large lumps.

3 Roughly crush **1⅓ cups fresh blackberries.** Mix ⅓ **cup plain yogurt** and ½ **cup crème fraîche (or plain yogurt)** and the **grated rind of ½ lemon.** Stir in **1 tablespoon clear honey.**

4 Layer the blackberries and oats with the yogurt mixture in 4 glasses. Chill for 1–2 hours. **serves 4**

NUTRITIONAL CONTENT PER 100 G: energy 25 calories | **protein** 0.9 g | **carbohydrates** 5 g | **fat** 0.2 g | **fiber** 7 g | **vitamin C** 15 mg | **vitamin E** 2.37 mg | **potassium** 160 mg | **calcium** 41 mg

strawberries

A daily portion of strawberries can help ward off infections and keep your heart healthy by raising blood folate levels, which helps to reduce the buildup of the harmful amino acid homocysteine in the blood, and by reducing systolic blood pressure. Strawberries may also have antiaging properties.

The fruits has some of the same disease-fighting antioxidants as raspberries, including ellagic acid, which combats carcinogens, and anthocyanidins, which have **anticancer**, **antimicrobial** and **anti-inflammatory** properties. Their antioxidant phenols may help ease arthritis and asthma, while the proanthocyanidins are thought to help keep the urinary tract and the heart healthy.

High levels of dietary fiber mean that strawberries are good for cleansing the digestive system and can reduce the risk of intestinal disorders as well as high blood pressure, diabetes, and heart disease.

✱ storing and serving For the best flavor, buy strawberries in season instead of those imported from abroad, and use them as soon as possible. Wash before hulling to prevent saturating their insides.

strawberry and cucumber salad

1 Halve **1 cucumber** lengthways, remove the seeds, and slice thinly. Place in a bowl with **1⅔ cups strawberries,** hulled and halved, or quartered if large.

2 Mix together **1 tablespoon balsamic vinegar, 1 teaspoon coarse-grain mustard, 1 teaspoon clear honey** and **3 tablespoons olive oil.** Season with **pepper.** Pour over the cucumber and strawberries.

3 Toss lightly to coat with the dressing and chill for 5–10 minutes before serving.
serves 4–6

NUTRITIONAL CONTENT PER 100 G: energy 27 calories | **protein** 1 g | **carbohydrates** 6 g | **fat** 0 g | **fiber** 2 g | **vitamin C** 77 mg | **potassium** 160 mg | **calcium** 16 mg | **magnesium** 10 mg | **iron** 0.4 mg

black currants

Black currants are one of the **richest sources of vitamin C** and canned black currants contain nearly as much vitamin C as fresh ones.

A general immunity-boosting nutrient, vitamin C also helps protect against strokes, heart disease, and cancer. The bioflavonoids in the fruit support the production of vitamin C, and these compounds work together to improve poor circulation and protect arterial health, thus helping maintain a healthy heart.

Black currants are powerful antioxidants and have **anti-inflammatory** and **antimicrobial** qualities, so they can help protect heart health, soothe kidney and bladder infections, and ward off cold sores and flu. They also have anti-laxative properties. Research suggests that the anthocyanidins and polyphenols may also help protect against Alzheimer's disease.

Closely related to black currants, **red currants** contain a good amount of the antioxidant anthocyanidins but much less vitamin C. Red currants are believed to help with arthritis, cystitis, and constipation and are great for cleansing the blood.

✱ **storing and serving** Add fresh currants to fruit salads or use them in jellies, jams, and preserves. They freeze well and can be used in juices.

blackcurrant water ice

1 Put **4½ cups (1 pound) black currants** in a pan with **2 tablespoons water.** Simmer until tender. Sieve to make 2½ cups puree.

2 Gently heat ½ **cup sugar** in ⅔ **cup water,** stirring until dissolved. Bring to a boil and simmer for 5 minutes. Let cool. Add the syrup to the puree with **2 tablespoons lemon juice.** Tip into a freezerproof container, cover, seal, and freeze.

3 When half-frozen, fold in **1 lightly whisked egg white.** Freeze until firm. Transfer to the refrigerator 15 minutes before serving to soften. **serves 4**

cranberries

Cranberries are **antioxidant powerhouses;** their phytonutrients help promote good heart health, inhibit cancerous cell growth, and counter premature aging.

A number of compounds peculiar to cranberries, including some of their proanthocyanidins, are responsible for the unique role of this fruit in **keeping the urinary system healthy.** They combat bacteria and viruses in the kidneys, bladder, and urinary tract by preventing bacteria, such as *E. coli,* from adhering to the walls of the urinary tract, so they are ideal for people with urinary problems, such as cystitis.

Similar anti-adhesion activity elsewhere in the body accounts for the effectiveness of cranberries in preventing listeria and *Helicobacter pylori* from causing gastrointestinal problems and oral bacteria from causing tooth decay. Cranberries can also help chesty coughs and sore throats.

✱ storing and serving Fresh cranberries will last for about two weeks in the refrigerator. Frozen fruit will keep for a year. Too sharp to eat raw, cranberries are ideal combined with naturally sweeter fruits, such as apples, and cooked to make jams and sauces.

cranberry muffins

1 Beat together **1 egg, ½ cup milk,** and **6 tablespoons softened unsalted butter.**

2 Sift together **1½ cups all-purpose flour** and **3 teaspoons baking powder** and stir into the mixture with **½ cup sugar.** Partially thaw **¾ cup (3 ounces) frozen cranberries** and stir in.

3 Spoon into a greased and lined 15-section muffin pan. Sprinkle **2 tablespoons sugar** and **1 teaspoon ground cinnamon** over the muffins. Bake in a preheated oven set to 350°F, for 20 minutes. Let cool in the pan for 2–3 minutes, then serve at once. **makes 15**

NUTRITIONAL CONTENT PER 100 G: energy 15 calories l **protein** 0.4 g l **carbohydrates** 3 g l **fat** 0 g l **fiber** 4 g l **vitamin C** 13 mg l **potassium** 95 mg l **calcium** 12 mg l **magnesium** 7 mg l **iron** 0.7 mg

cherries

Like all berries, cherries are a good source of antioxidants, particularly the anthocyanidins.

As well as helping **prevent or repair the damage done by free radicals,** the flavonoids in cherries help joint health. Research shows that these antioxidants inhibit inflammation-causing enzymes and reduce the levels of uric acid in painful joints. Eating cherries daily can help alleviate inflammatory disorders, such as gout and rheumatoid arthritis, as well as relieveing headaches and migraine. Cherries contain several **anticancer** compounds, including ellagic acid.

Melatonin, a hormone produced in the brain's pineal gland and also found in significant quantities in cherries, may prevent or reduce age-related brain deterioration. Melatonin also aids the body's natural sleep patterns and may help deal with insomnia.

Cherries have a very low glycaemic index, so a handful of cherries is an ideal snack, stabilizing blood sugar levels and keeping hunger at bay.

✱ storing and serving Choose fruit on the stem to discourage decay and refrigerate for up to a week. Canned and bottled cherries retain many nutritients.

cherry clafoutis

1 Make a batter by mixing together ¾ **cup all-purpose flour, 2 tablespoons sugar, 3 eggs, 1 cup milk,** and a **few drops of vanilla extract**.

2 Grease a 1½-quart soufflé dish with **1 tablespoon butter,** heat for a few minutes, then add **2½ cups (1 pound) pitted black cherries** together with any juice. Cover with the batter.

3 Bake the clafoutis in a preheated oven set to 400°F, for 30 minutes, or until well risen. Dust with **powdered sugar** and serve at once. **serves 4**

NUTRITIONAL CONTENT PER 100 G WITH PITS: energy 39 calories I **protein** 1 g I **carbohydrates** 10 g I **fat** 0 g I **fiber** 1 g I **vtamin C** 9 mgI **potassium** 170 mg I **calcium** 11 mg

83

plums and prunes

Fresh and dried plums (prunes) contain many of the disease-protective phytonutrients that help neutralize the damaging free radicals related to accelerated aging and DNA degradation. They are also rich in **potassium,** which is essential for maintaining normal blood pressure and heart function and the growth and repair of lean body tissue.

Converting plums into prunes concentrates the nutrients in the dried fruit; prunes are thought to have **more than twice the antioxidant power** of the "super food" blueberries. The high fiber content of prunes and a bowel-stimulating chemical called hydroxyphenylisatin account for their laxative qualities and their role in reducing the risk of cancers, particularly of the bowel. The fiber in prunes is good for cholesterol levels, which maintains heart health.

Like all dried fruit, prunes boost energy. They also contain boron, which benefits menopausal women.

✱ **storing and serving** Don't avoid fresh plums with a slight whitish bloom—this is a good indicator that the fruit has not been overhandled. Let plums ripen in the fruit bowl, then refrigerate.

hot fruit salad

1 Let **1 cup prunes**, **1 cup dried figs** and **1 cup dried apricots** soak in **2½ cups apple juice** overnight.

2 Transfer to a saucepan and simmer for 10–15 minutes.

3 Turn into a bowl and pour over **2 tablespoons Calvados** (or brandy), if you want. Sprinkle with **¼ cup coarsely chopped walnuts** and serve with **plain yogurt,** if you want. **serves 6**

NUTRITIONAL CONTENT PER 100 G PLUMS WITH PITS (PRUNES NO PITS): energy 34 (140) calories | **protein** 1 (3) g | **carbohydrates** 8 (34) g | **fat** 0 (0) g | **fiber** 2 (13) g | **iron** 0.4 (2.6) mg

85

dates

Dates, especially dried ones, are a particularly sweet and satisfying food, thanks to their natural sugar and fiber content. The fiber moderates the speed at which energy from the sugars is released, so that dates make a **good energizing food** for snacks and for eating both before and after exercise. The fiber content also gives dates laxative properties, while the natural sugars have a soothing influence by helping to raise levels of the calming serotonin in the brain.

Dates contain beta-carotene, vitamins B_6 and B_3 **(niacin),** which help maintain healthy skin and the nervous and digestive systems. The niacin makes dates good for those who have depression.

The **iron** in dates means they are useful for anyone who has fatigue or anemia. Dates also contain some **potassium,** which helps regulate blood pressure, and magnesium, vital for bones, muscles, and the heart.

✱ storing and serving Dates are available both fresh and dried, with or without stones. Keep them in sealed plastic bags or airtight containers in the refrigerator. Some fresh dates will keep for several months, and dried dates can be kept for up to a year.

date and orange fool

1 Squeeze the juice from **2 large oranges** and make up the quantity to 1¼ cups with water. Place in a pan with ¾ **cup pitted dates.** Bring to a boil, cover, and simmer for 10 minutes or until soft.

2 Cool slightly, then process in a blender until smooth. Set aside until cold.

3 Put alternate spoonfuls of date puree and 1¼ **cups plain yogurt** in 4 small dishes. Swirl together attractively with a small knife.

4 Chill until required, then serve topped with **sliced banana. serves 4**

NUTRITIONAL CONTENT PER 100 G DRIED DATES WITH PITS: energy 227 calories I **protein** 3 g I **carbohydrates** 57 g I **fat** 0 g I **fiber** 7 g I **potassium** 590 mg I **calcium** 38 mg

watermelons

The red flesh is a clue that watermelon is a rich source of lycopene, the antioxidant carotenoid that is found in tomatoes and is believed to reduce the risk of several cancers, particularly prostate cancer.

Like cantaloupe melons, watermelons are **high in vitamin C and beta-carotene** (vitamin A). The action of these antioxidants in disarming the dangerous free radicals that roam the body causing damage and premature aging helps protect against stroke, certain cancers, and heart disease. They also help maintain youthful-looking skin and encourage a **healthy immune system** and good vision; they have **anti-inflammatory** properties and may help alleviate some symptoms of asthma and rheumatoid arthritis.

The **potassium** in watermelons helps regulate blood pressure and maintain the body's fluid balance. Like all melons, watermelons are natural diuretics and a good choice for anyone who has water retention.

✱ **storing and serving** A whole watermelon can be stored at room temperature if it's not too warm, but it is best refrigerated. Once cut open, refrigerate watermelon wrapped tightly in plastic.

watermelon and feta salad

1 Dry-fry **1 tablespoon black sesame seeds** for a few minutes until aromatic.

2 Arrange **3 cups (1 pound) peeled and diced watermelon** and **1½ cups diced feta cheese** on a plate with **2 cups arugula** and a few **herb sprigs.**

3 Whisk **6 tablespoons olive oil, 1 tablespoon pomegranate syrup, 1 tablespoon orange flower juice, 1½ tablespoons lemon juice,** and **½ teaspoon sugar.** Season with **salt and pepper** and drizzle over the salad. Scatter over the sesame seeds and serve with toasted **pita bread. serves 4 as a starter**

NUTRITIONAL CONTENT PER 100 G FLESH: energy 31 calories | **protein** 1 g | **carbohydrates** 7 g | **fat** 0 g | **fiber** 0 g | **vitamin C** 8 mg | **potassium** 100 mg | **magnesium** 8 mg

cantaloupe melons

These orange-fleshed melons, also known as musk melons, are excellent sources of beta-carotene and vitamin C. These nutrients are **powerful antioxidants,** which neutralize the free radicals that cause heart disease, cancer, and premature aging. In addition, they help maintain healthy, youthful skin by encouraging skin cell turnover and maintaining the elasticity and plumpness of the skin. Beta-carotene may also provide protection from within against damage to the skin from ultraviolet rays.

In addition, vitamin A helps maintain healthy vision and vitamin C is well known for its role in boosting the **immune system,** so a diet that regularly includes cantaloupe melon offers many health benefits, including helping reduce the risk of cataracts and macular degeneration and helping fight infection.

Thanks to their high **potassium** content—higher even than the potassium-rich banana—cantaloupes are good for the heart. The potassium helps regulate blood pressure and eliminate "bad" cholesterol.

✳ **storing and serving** Store ripe melons and cut melons in the refrigerator. Wrap the latter or store in an airtight container to prevent the ethylene gas they give off from affecting other fruits and vegetables.

melon with raspberries

1 Cut **2 baby cantaloupe melons** in half and scoop out and discard the seeds.

2 Spoon **1 cup raspberries** into the hollows and top up with **1¼ cups chilled Monbazillac or other sweet whie wine.** Chill for at least 15 minutes before serving. **serves 4**

NUTRITIONAL CONTENT PER 100 G: calories 17 calories I protein 1 g I carbohydrate 3 g I fiber 1 g I **vitamin C** 17 mg I **vitamin E** 1.2 mg I **potassium** 256 mg I **calcium** 7 mg I **magnesium** 7 mg

tomatoes

A key ingredient in the Mediterranean diet, an area famed for its low incidence of heart disease, tomatoes contain beta-carotene, vitamins C and E and **zinc.** These antioxidants help **strengthen the immune system** and reduce the risk of cataracts and other eye problems, heart disease, strokes, and some cancers.

Tomatoes, the redder and riper the better, are a good source of the antioxidant lycopene, which is associated with a reduced risk of prostate and breast cancers and heart disease. Unusually for fruits and vegetables, consuming cooked or processed tomatoes, such as canned tomatoes and tomato paste, is even more beneficial than eating fresh ones.

In addition, tomatoes contain high levels of salicylates, which prevent thickening of the blood, and zinc, which is vital for fertility, especially in men. Tomatoes may help to soothe inflammation of the liver, and their high-water content helps the digestive system to function efficiently.

✽ **choosing and serving** There are numerous varieties of tomato. Sun-ripened tomatoes are the best choice, because they contain more lycopene and have a sweeter, fuller flavor than those ripened under glass. Plum tomatoes are best for cooking.

tomato and cilantro salsa

1 Finely chop **1 red onion** and deseed and chop **3 medium vine-ripened tomatoes.** Mix with **2 crushed garlic cloves** and **2–3 tablespoons chopped fresh cilantro leaves.**

2 Season lightly with **salt and pepper,** cover, and chill for at least 30 minutes to allow the flavors to develop.

3 Serve the salsa with cold meats or as a side dish with Indian dishes and other spicy food. **makes about ½ cup**

93

corn

Corn, also known as maize and sweet corn, is a particularly good source of fiber and some B vitamins, including B_1 (thiamin), B_3 (niacin) and B_5 (pantotheic acid), which help with energy production. Vitamin B_5 is especially useful when the body is experiencing stress, while thiamin also helps preserve the memory. Another B vitamin found in high levels is **folate,** which helps prevent birth defects, improve the blood, and protect the heart.

The fiber in corn helps **reduce high blood cholesterol levels** and protect against bowel cancer. The fiber also helps it release its energy slowly without disrupting blood sugar levels, making corn a good vegetable for diabetics.

The carotenoid zeaxanthin, which accounts for the yellow color and is unaffected by the canning process, helps maintain healthy eyesight and protect against lung and breast cancers.

✱ **storing and serving** Choose corn with fresh-looking green husks and soft, moist silk. Warmth converts the sugar to starch, so refrigerate and eat as soon as possible. Freeze cobs and bottle the kernels.

corn cakes

1 Finely shred **4 lime leaves** and blend with ½ **cup plus 2 tablespoons all-purpose flour, 1 egg, 1 tablespoon Thai fish sauce, 1 tablespoon lime juice,** and ⅔ **cup corn kernels** until fairly smooth.

2 Stir in another ⅔ **cup corn kernels.** Heat **2 inches vegetable oil** in a wok and deep-fry teaspoons of the batter, in batches, for 1–2 minutes, or until golden. Drain on paper towel and keep warm while you cook the remainder.

3 Place a corn cake on each of **24 chicory spears,** top with a few **herb sprigs** (such as basil, mint, or fresh cilantro), and serve immediately. **makes about 24**

NUTRITIONAL CONTENT PER 100 G KERNELS ONLY: energy 12 calories I **protein** 3 g I **carbohydrates** 12 g I **fat** 1 g I **fiber** 2.5 g I **vitamin C** 4 mg I **potassium** 140 mg I **magnesium** 20 mg

avocados

Nutrient-rich avocados are often shunned because of their high-fat content. However, much of this fat is the monounsaturated variety and is easily digested, with none of the artery-clogging effects of saturated fat.

Avocados are **rich in the antioxidant vitamins** (A, C, and E) that protect cells from the damage inflicted by free radicals and are useful for preventing conditions such as heart disease. The **vitamin E** content also means that avocado helps maintain healthy skin and circulation. Not only does eating avocado provide its own antioxidants, it also improves the absorption of antioxidants from other fruits and vegetables eaten at the same time.

Avocados are good sources of the blood pressure-regulator **potassium** and the energizing B vitamins, in particular the "anti-stress" vitamin B_5, essential for adrenal function, making them great for helping your body cope naturally with the effects of ongoing stress.

✻ storing and serving Most avocados reach the supermarket in an unripened form. As they ripen, they start to lose important antioxidant nutrients, especially vitamin C, so eat as soon as they are ripe.

avocado salsa

1 Peel, pit, and finely dice **2 small ripe avocados.**

2 Finely chop **8 scallions** and combine with the avocados, **2 tablespoons lemon juice,** and **2 tablespoons chopped fresh cilantro.** Season with **salt and pepper** and serve. **makes about ½ cup**

NUTRITIONAL CONTENT PER 100 G FLESH: energy 190 calories | **protein** 2 g | **carbohydrates** 2 g | **fat** 20 g | **fiber** 3 g | **vitamin C** 6 mg | **potassium** 450 mg | **magnesium** 25 mg

onions

Onions are a **good source of many powerful antioxidants,** which neutralize the cell-damaging free radicals in the body, helping to reduce the risk of strokes, heart disease, cancer, Alzheimer's disease and the other degenerative diseases of aging. Chief among these is quercetin, which is plentiful in red onions and protects against heart disease by preventing furred arteries and blood clots from forming.

The sulfurous compounds in onions—the ones that cause tears when you slice onions—when eaten daily will help reduce high blood pressure and high cholesterol levels and may help protect against asthma and some inflammatory disorders, such as rheumatoid arthritis. These compounds, also found in garlic, are thought to fight cancer and **stimulate the liver's own natural detoxification process.** Indeed, research has shown that those who eat a lot of onions have lower rates of stomach cancer.

✱ **storing and serving** Onions can be stored for several weeks at room temperature in a dry, well-ventilated basket or vegetable rack out of direct sunlight. Keep scallions in the refrigerator.

smooth onion soup

1 Finely chop **4 large onions** and cook gently in **3 tablespoons olive oil** for 20 minutes, stirring occasionally.

2 When the onions are soft and golden-brown, add **5 cups vegetable stock** and **2 teaspoons chopped thyme** and bring to a boil. Boil for 2 minutes, then reduce the heat, cover, and simmer for 30 minutes. Add **salt and pepper** to taste.

3 Blend the soup until smooth, then return to the pan and reheat gently. Add **1 tablespoon chopped parsley** before serving. **serves 4**

NUTRITIONAL CONTENT PER 100 G: energy 36 calories I **protein** 1 g I **carbohydrates** 8 g I **fat** 0 g I **fiber** 1.5 g I **vitamin C** 5 mg I **potassium** 160 mg I **calcium** 25 mg I **magnesium** 4 mg

broccoli

The name broccoli is applied to both white- and purple-sprouting broccoli and calabrese, the green heads sold in supermarkets. They are **powerhouses of nutrition** and should be eaten between one and three times a week for their many health-giving qualities.

All types of broccoli are rich in sulforaphane and indoles. These stimulate the production of enzymes that help neutralize cancer-causing substances in the body and are a **major force in protecting against cancer,** particularly bowel cancer.

Broccoli also protects against heart disease and respiratory infections. It stimulates the liver, making the whole body function better, including the skin. Broccoli is a good source of **folate,** vital for hemoglobin formation, thus helping prevent anemia.

Folic acid and tryptophan, an amino acid, also promote the production of the "feel-good" neurotransmitter serotonin, so broccoli may benefit people suffering from depression and insomnia.

✱ **storing and serving** Store in the refrigerator and use within a day or so. Eat small florets raw, or boil, steam, microwave, or stir-fry. Do not overcook.

broccoli sabzi

1 Stir-fry **1 teaspoon cumin seeds** in **2 tablespoons vegetable oil.** Finely slice **1 onion** and add to the pan. Cook until lightly browned.

2 Finely slice **1 red chili pepper** and **3 garlic cloves** and add to the pan with **1¼ cups broccoli,** divided into small florets. Cover, reduce the heat, and cook for 6–8 minutes, until the broccoli is just tender.

3 Season with **salt and pepper** and serve hot with a spicy Indian dish. **serves 4**

NUTRITIONAL CONTENT PER 100 G: energy 33 calories I **protein** 4 g I **carbohydrates** 2 g I **fat** 1 g I **fiber** 3 g I **vitamin C** 87 mg I **carotene** 535 mcg I **folate** 90 mcg I **potassium** 370 mg

seaweed

Technically algae, edible seaweed is the richest food source of the mineral **iodine,** essential for normal functioning of the thyroid gland and which may help prevent breast cancer. It is also rich in **folate,** which is good for preventing birth defects and linked to a reduced risk of bowel cancer.

Seaweed is great for heart health because the folate helps protect against heart disease and stroke, while its magnesium content helps reduce high blood pressure and heart attack. In addition, magnesium's action as a natural relaxant means that eating seaweed may help reduce the severity of asthma symptoms, prevent migraines, and provide some relief from menopausal symptoms.

Including seaweed in the diet may also provide some protection from hormone-dependent cancers, because the lignans (plant compounds) in seaweed have cancer-fighting properties.

Another type of algae, which is available in powdered form, **spirulina** is commonly used in juices for its energizing and health-boosting properties.

✱ **storing and serving** Increasingly available in health-food stores and good supermarkets, seaweeds can be kept in airtight containers for several months.

seaweed and cucumber salad

1 Put **1 ounce mixed dried seaweed** (such as dulse or sea lettuce) in a bowl, cover with cold water, and let stand for 15–20 minutes.

2 Cut **1 small cucumber** in half lengthways and slice thinly. Drain the seaweed and roughly chop any large pieces. Put the chopped seaweed in a bowl with the sliced cucumber and toss lightly. Serve as an accompaniment to broiled fish. **serves 4**

asparagus

Eat plenty of asparagus if you are trying to conceive or are in the early stages of pregnancy because it contains a lot of **folate,** which protects against neural tube defects in the unborn baby.

The potassium-sodium balance in asparagus, combined with an amino acid called asparagine, has a **diuretic effect,** so eating asparagus is good for liver and kidney function and may help alleviate bloating during menstruation.

Powerful antioxidants in asparagus—vitamins C and E and glutathione—help reduce the risk of cancer, heart disease, and age-related degenerative diseases. Asparagus also contains detoxifying glucosinolates and is a source of vitamin K, which promotes blood clotting.

Avoid eating asparagus if you suffer from gout because it contains purines, which increase the uric acid in the joints and exacerbate the condition.

✳ storing and serving Asparagus stalks should be straight and firm with dark, tightly furled tips. The stalk should break without bending. Keep asparagus refrigerated and try to eat on the day of purchase because flavor and vitamins quickly diminish. Serve cooked with melted butter, as Julius Caesar liked it.

hot asparagus with balsamic vinegar dressing

1 Skin, deseed, and finely chop **2–3 medium tomatoes** and mix with **2 tablespoons balsamic vinegar, 1–2 cloves crushed garlic,** and **5 tablespoons olive oil.** Set aside.

2 Trim **16–20 (1 pound) young asparagus spears,** arrange them in a single layer on a preheated, medium griddle pan, and cook for 5 minutes, turning constantly.

3 Transfer the asparagus to 4 warm plates. Spoon over the dressing and top with ½ **cup toasted pine nuts** and ¼ **cup Parmesan shavings.** Season and serve at once. **serves 4**

NUTRITIONAL CONTENT PER 100 G: energy 25 calories I **protein** 3 g I **carbohydrates** 2 g I **fat** 1 g I **fiber** 2 g I **vitamin C** 12 mg I **folate** 175 mcg I **potassium** 260 mg I **calcium** 27 mg

105

peas

Fresh peas are one of the richest fresh vegetable sources of **iron** and also contain a good amount of vitamin B_1 (thiamin). The iron can help prevent anemia, while the thiamin is required to convert food into energy and help maintain a healthy heart and nervous system.

The soluble fiber in peas makes them a **good choice for diabetics** because it both slows down the release of energy and stabilizes blood sugar levels. The fiber also helps protect the heart by reducing cholesterol levels.

The green pigment in peas, chlorophyllin, can help prevent cancer because it carries free radicals out of the body. Plant hormones, lignans, are thought to protect against hormone-dependent cancers as well as menopausal problems.

The carotenoids lutein and zaethanin help maintain healthy eyes, and **folate** can help prevent birth defects and helping reduce the risk of heart disease.

✱ **storing and serving** Fresh peas need to be kept in the refrigerator to preserve their texture, flavor and nutrients. They are best eaten on the day of purchase. Frozen peas are as good, or better, a source as fresh ones for vitamin C.

summer green pea soup

1 Trim, wash, and chop a **bunch of scallions** and soften in **1 tablespoon butter**. Do not allow them to color.

2 Shell **2½ pounds fresh peas** (or use 3½ cups/1 pound frozen peas) and add them to the pan with **3 cups vegetable stock.** Bring to the boil and simmer for about 15 minutes (5 minutes for frozen peas).

3 Blend the soup until smooth and return to the pan. Stir in **2 tablespoons plain yogurt,** reheat gently, and serve, sprinkled with **1 tablespoon chopped chives. serves 4**

green beans

The term green beans covers all types of thick or skinny, long, fresh beans with small seeds inside.

Eating green beans **helps maintain bone strength** because they are a great source of vitamin K. They also contain many nutrients with heart-protective qualities, including the antioxidant vitamins A and C, which **neutralize damaging free radicals** and help prevent clogged arteries; potassium and magnesium, which work together to **lower high blood pressure;** folate, which protects against heart attack, and stroke by preventing the harmful buildup of the amino acid homocysteine; and soluble fiber, which helps **lower blood cholesterol.**

The fiber in beans helps keep the digestive system healthy and prevent bowel cancer by removing toxins from the body. Richer in **iron** than spinach, green beans can help prevent fatigue and anemia.

✱ **storing and serving** Green beans keep in the refrigerator for a few days. Blanch and use in salads or with dips, or steam or stir-fry them. Canned and frozen beans retain about half their original vitamin C content.

green bean and tomato salad

1 Halve **4 red and yellow baby plum tomatoes** and put them in a large bowl.

2 Cook **1½ cups trimmed thin green beans**, for 2 minutes, drain well, and add to the tomatoes.

3 Add a **handful of chopped mint, 1 crushed garlic clove, 4 tablespoons olive oil,** and **1 tablespoon balsamic vinegar.** Season with **salt and pepper** and mix well. Serve warm or cold. **serves 4**

NUTRITIONAL CONTENT PER 100 G: energy 24 calories | **protein** 2 g | **carbohydrates** 3 g | **fat** 1 g | **fiber** 3 g | **vitamin C** 12 mg | **folate** 80 mcg | **potassium** 230 mg | **calcium** 36 mg | **iron** 1.2 mg

109

fava beans

Archaeological evidence suggests that fava beans, also known as broad, faba, horse, and Windsor beans, were cultivated in Neolithic times, making them one of the first crops to be cultivated.

A good source of protein, they are ideal for vegetarians. The fiber they contain helps keep the digestive system healthy, so helps **protect against bowel cancer** and **lower blood cholesterol levels.**

Fava beans are a good choice for women in the early stages of pregnancy because they contain **folate.** And they are good for controlling blood pressure because their **potassium** helps regulate fluid levels in the body.

Fava beans are known to provoke a severe allergic reaction called favism in a small group of people of Mediterranean or Middle Eastern origin—where the bean originated.

✱ **storing and serving** To avoid flavor loss, keep fava beans in the refrigerator and use as soon as possible. The pods of young fava beans are edible.

fava bean and pecorino salad

1 Shell **12 ounces fresh fava beans** and blanch in boiling water for 2 minutes. Drain and refresh. If you have time, after blanching the beans, remove the outer skins to reveal the bright green, velvety bean inside.

2 Coarsely grate **6 ounces pecorino or Parmesan cheese** and put it in a mixing bowl. Add the beans, **2 tablespoons each of olive oil** and **lemon juice,** and **1 tablespoon chopped flat-leaf parsley.** Season with **salt and pepper** and mix well. Serve as part of an antipasto. **serves 4**

NUTRITIONAL CONTENT PER 100 G: energy 59 calories | **protein** 6 g | **carbohydrates** 7 g | **fat** 1 g | **fiber** 6 g | **vitamin C** 32 mg | **folate** 145 mcg | **potassium** 310 mg | **calcium** 23 mg

snow peas

Snow peas, also known as mangetout, are flat, wide, edible pods with little bulges indicating the small, immature peas. Their nutritional profile is similar to that of green peas, although the immature seeds account for some differences—there is less protein in snow peas, for example. However, they provide twice the **calcium** and slightly more **iron** than green peas and are a better source of beta-carotene (vitamin A).

The iron and **folate** in snow peas can help build red blood cells so snow peas are good for people susceptible to anemia. Folate can also help prevent birth defects. In addition, it may help keep heart and blood vessels healthy.

The fiber in snow peas also helps prevent cancer by keeping the digestive system working efficiently, and it can protect the heart by **reducing blood cholesterol levels.**

✱ **storing and serving** Keep snow peas in the refrigerator and use as soon as possible after purchase. Eat them raw or only slightly cooked to retain some "crunch" as well as their nutrients; they are ideal in stir-fries or they can be steamed. Rinse before cooking and trim the ends off the pods.

snow peas with ginger and mint

1 Cut **2 inches fresh piece of ginger root** into matchsticks and stir-fry in **2 tablespoons olive oil** for 1–2 minutes to flavor the oil.

2 Trim **5 cups (1 pound) snow peas**, add to the pan and stir-fry for 2 minutes.

3 Remove from the heat and stir in **2 teaspoons lemon juice** and **2 tablespoons chopped mint.** Season to taste with **salt and pepper** and serve at once, garnished with **mint sprigs. serves 4–6**

NUTRITIONAL CONTENT PER 100 G RAW: energy 32 calories | **protein** 4 g | **carbohydrates** 4 g | **fat** 0 g | **fiber** 4 g | **vitamin C** 21 mg | **potassium** 200 mg | **calcium** 44 mg | **iron** 0.8 mg

113

okra

Also known as bindi and lady's fingers, okra is a member of the cotton family and originated in Africa. It is a green (sometimes white), tapering seed capsule and has its own unique flavor and texture.

Okra is high in dietary fiber, which helps keep the digestive system healthy and protects the heart by **lowering high blood cholesterol levels.** Okra contains even more **potassium** than bananas and this can help regulate fluid levels in the body and is, therefore, important for controlling blood pressure.

Okra is also a good source of vitamin C—essential for boosting immunity and for general good health—and a number of B vitamins, including **folate.** Taken by mothers-to-be, folic acid can help protect babies from neural tube defects. It also boosts red blood cells, helping to combat fatigue and anemia.

✱ storing and serving Choose small, young pods that have not yet matured and toughened. Once cut, okra oozes a slimy sap, which is ideal for thickening soups and stews but is not to everyone's taste. To minimize this sap, cut okra only just before cooking and cook it quickly.

bhindi bhaji

1 Heat **3 tablespoons vegetable oil** and add **1 tablespoon mustard seeds** and **1 tablespoon cumin seeds.**

2 Trim **1 pound okra** and cut into ½-inch slices. When the mustard seeds begin to pop, add the okra and stir-fry for 8–10 minutes.

3 Add **1 teaspoon chili powder, 1 tablespoon dhana-jeera, 2 teaspoons jaggery** (or soft brown sugar), and **1 finely chopped tomato** and cook for 3–5 minutes. Remove from the heat, season with **salt and pepper,** and stir in **2 tablespoons chopped fresh cilantro.** Serve hot with **lime wedges**, if you want. **serves 4**

NUTRITIONAL CONTENT PER 100 G RAW: energy 31 calories I **protein** 3 g I **carbohydrates** 3 g I **fat** 1 g I **fiber** 5 g I **vitamin C** 21 mg I **folate** 88 mcg I **potassium** 330 mg I **calcium** 160 mg

bell peppers

Red, yellow, and orange bell peppers are simply riper versions of green ones, and their longer maturing time increases their overall nutrient content.

All bell peppers, especially red ones, contain high levels of the antioxidants vitamin C, beta-carotene (vitamin A), **vitamin E,** and **zinc,** so they fight off free radicals and protect against heart disease, strokes, and some cancers. These same nutrients are vital for a **strong immune system** and for energy production.

Vitamin C and the magnesium in peppers work together to produce adrenaline, which makes peppers great for helping the body deal with stress.

Red peppers contain the red carotenoid lycopene, which helps prevent prostate cancer, and lutein and zeaxanthin, which both protect against vision problems, such as cataracts and macular degeneration.

Other chemicals in bell peppers help prevent constipation, if drunk in fresh juice or eaten raw.

✱ **storing and serving** Choose firm, unwrinkled peppers and store in the refrigerator. All colors can be eaten raw or cooked and can even be juiced.

roasted stuffed bell peppers

1 Halve, core, and deseed **4 large red bell peppers**. Put the peppers, cut sides up, in a ceramic dish. Scatter over **2 crushed garlic cloves** and **1 tablespoon chopped thyme** and season with **salt and pepper.**

2 Halve **4 plum tomatoes** and put a piece in each pepper. Drizzle with a mixture of **4 tablespoons olive oil** and **2 tablespoons balsamic vinegar** and roast in a preheated oven set to 425°F, for 55–60 minutes or until the peppers are soft and charred. Serve with crusty bread and a baby leaf salad. **serves 4**

NUTRITIONAL CONTENT PER 100 G RED RAW: energy 32 calories | **protein** 1 g | **carbohydrates** 6 g | **fat** 0 g | **fiber** 2 g | **vitamin C** 140 mg | **carotene** 3840 mcg | **potassium** 160 mg

117

118

carrots

Carrots are probably the richest vegetable source of carotenoids. These antioxidants and the other nutrients in carrots—fiber, **calcium, potassium,** magnesium, vitamins C and E, among others—give the vegetable plenty of health-boosting powers.

Carrots are vital for the **immune system** and protect against heart and arterial diseases and cancer. They also help regulate blood sugar levels and **reduce blood cholesterol** levels, and they are vital for building strong teeth, hair, and bones. Easy to digest and good for internal cleansing, carrots have beneficial effects on the digestive system and skin as well as on the respiratory system.

The beta-carotene in carrots is also believed to promote good eyesight, especially night vision. In addition, beta-carotene, lutein, and zeaxanthin help to **protect the eyes** from ultraviolet light and reduce the risk of cataracts and macular degeneration.

✱ **storing and serving** Store carrots in a plastic bag in the refrigerator, first removing their green tops if they are still attached to prevent them from drying out. Scrub carrots well and, unless they are organic, peel them to avoid ingesting pesticide residues. Juicing is a popular way to benefit from the goodness in carrots.

carrot and cilantro pâté

1 Grate **5–7 medium carrots** and put them in a saucepan with **1 tablespoon ground coriander,** ¾ **cup orange juice** and 1¼ **cups water.** Cover and simmer for 40 minutes, or until the carrots are cooked. Let cool.

2 Drain quickly and transfer to a food processor with a little of the cooking liquid. Add ½ **cup reduced-fat soft cheese** and 1¼ **cups fresh cilantro.** Blend until smooth, season with **salt and pepper,** and blend again.

3 Chill and serve with whole-grain bread or toast. **serves 4**

fennel

Florence fennel, the swollen, bulb-like leaf base of a relative of the herb fennel, contains **phytoestrogens,** compounds produced naturally in plants that mimic the female hormone estrogen. Women may, therefore, find fennel useful for dealing with premenstrual syndrome (PMS) and for relieving some menopausal symptoms, such as hot flashes. Phytoestrogens are also thought to offer some protection against hormone-related cancers.

Fennel contains a good range of antioxidants, including two flavonoids, quercetin and rutin, and vitamin C, which means that fennel has **anticancer** and **antimicrobial** properties and that it provides a good boost to the **immune system.**

The **potassium** and fiber in fennel are great for the health of the heart and digestive system. Fiber also helps reduce the risk of bowel cancer.

✱ **storing and serving** Florence fennel has a distinctive aniseed flavor. It may be eaten raw in salads, or cooked, usually by braising, steaming, or baking. The leaves and seeds of the herbaceous perennial fennel are used as herbs and seasonings. Fennel tea is a useful digestive aid after a rich meal.

braised fennel with pecorino

1 Melt **4 tablespoons butter** in a large pan. When it stops foaming, add **12 baby fennel bulbs,** trimmed and halved lengthways, and fry gently for 2 minutes on each side until lightly golden. Add ⅔ **cup water** and a **squeeze of lemon juice.** Season with **salt and pepper,** bring to a boil, cover and simmer for 20 minutes, or until the fennel is tender.

2 Add **1 tablespoon balsamic vinegar** and increase the heat to reduce the liquid by half. Remove the pan from the heat, add **3–4 tablespoons grated pecorino cheese,** and allow the cheese to melt. Serve the fennel and pan juices with new potatoes. **serves 4**

NUTRITIONAL CONTENT PER 100 G RAW: energy 12 calories | **protein** 1 g | **carbohydrates** 2 g | **fat** 0 g | **fiber** 2 g | **vitamin C** 5 mg | **potassium** 440 mg | **calcium** 24 mg | **magnesium** 8 mg

121

spinach

Spinach is an important source of the antioxidants beta-carotene and vitamins C and E, which strengthen the **immune system** and reduce the risk of heart disease and stroke as well as some cancers. The carotenoids in spinach may also protect against cataracts and macular degeneration.

Although spinach is best known for its **high iron content,** these levels are not as high as once thought. Iron helps prevent fatigue and anemia.

The vitamin K and magnesium in spinach help **build healthy blood cells,** while the **calcium** builds bones and teeth and helps prevent osteoarthritis.

Spinach is a good source of **folate,** which builds up red blood cells and is essential in early pregnancy for helping to protect babies from spina bifida.

Spinach is also a natural laxative, but the oxalic acid in the leaves makes it unsuitable for people with kidney or bladder stones.

✱ storing and serving Spinach may be stored in a bag in the refrigerator for a few days. Wash the leaves then shake dry for use in a salad. Alternatively, steam quickly using just the water clinging to the leaves.

bacon, spinach, and blue cheese salad

1 Chop **3 slices of smoked Canadian-style bacon** and fry until crisp. Add ¼ **cup pine nuts** and cook for 1–2 minutes, until the nuts begin to brown.

2 Wash **4 cups fresh baby spinach,** dice ½ cup Gorgonzola **or other blue cheese,** and halve **12 cherry tomatoes** and stir into the bacon and pine nuts. Transfer the salad to a serving bowl.

3 Mix together **1 teaspoon whole-grain mustard, 1 teaspoon clear honey,** and **2 tablespoons balsamic vinegar.** Pour the dressing over the salad and serve with crusty bread. **serves 4**

NUTRITIONAL CONTENT PER 100 G FRESH, RAW: energy 25 calories I **protein** 3 g I **carbohydrates** 2 g I **fat** 1 g I **fiber** 4 g I **vitamin C** 26 mg I **carotene** 3535 mcg I **vitamin E** 1.7 mg

123

mushrooms

Classed as a fungus rather than a vegetable, mushrooms are an excellent source of **selenium,** an **anticancer** mineral that can limit the damage inflicted in the body by free radicals. Mushrooms are believed to offer protection against breast cancer, thanks to their part in regulating levels of estrogen in the body.

Fresh and dried mushrooms are rich in phytochemicals that protect the body when it is under stress, particularly vitamin B_5, which is essential for adrenal function and improves the body's coping mechanisms.

The **potassium** present in mushrooms helps regulate the body's fluid levels, including blood pressure.

Research has shown **oriental mushrooms** to be more health-boosting than common mushrooms. They are thought to help prevent blood clots. Shiitake and reishi mushrooms contain the phytochemical lentinan, believed to prevent and treat cancer and viral diseases as well as **reducing high blood cholesterol levels** and high blood pressure.

✱ **storing and serving** Keep white button mushrooms in the refrigerator in a paper bag for 1–2 days. Use wild mushrooms soon after purchase.

roast mushrooms on toast

1 Put **8 large mushrooms**, in a roasting pan and season with **salt and pepper.** In a bowl, mix together **2 crushed garlic cloves, ½ cup olive oil, 2 teaspoons chopped thyme,** and the finely grated rind of **1 lemon.** Spoon half of the sauce over the mushrooms.

2 Roast the mushrooms in a preheated oven set to 425°F, for 20 minutes. Drizzle over **4 tablespoons lemon juice.**

3 Put the mushrooms on 4 slices of **buttered toast,** drizzle over the remaining sauce, and serve topped with **arugula** and shavings of **Parmesan cheese. serves 4**

NUTRITIONAL CONTENT PER 100 G RAW: energy 13 calories I **protein** 2 g I **carbohydrates** 0 g I **fat** 1 g I **fiber** 2 g I **vitamin C** 1 mg I **potassium** 320 mg I **calcium** 6 mg I **selenium** 9 mcg

NUTRITIONAL CONTENT PER 100 G RAW: energy 114 calories I **protein** 2 g I **carbohydrates** 28 g I **fat** 0 g I **fiber** 4 g I vitamin C 4 mg I **vitamin B$_6$** 0.16 mg I **potassium** 380 mg I **manganese** 0.1 mg

yams

In the United States, the word yam is sometimes applied to sweet potatoes with yellow flesh, and yams are often confused with sweet potatoes, but they are different, unrelated vegetables. The hundreds of varieties account for yams' varying flesh and skin colors, which only add to the confusion. They are usually long and cylindrical, with rough, scaly skin.

The antioxidants **vitamin C** and **manganese** in yams provide protection against free radicals. Yams also contain a lot of **potassium** (even more than bananas) and vitamin B$_6$, two nutrients that help protect the heart. Potassium helps regulate blood pressure, so it is useful for dealing with hypertension, while vitamin B$_6$ breaks down homocysteine, a substance that can damage blood vessel walls resulting in strokes and heart attacks.

A good energizing food, yams release their carbohydrates slowly into the body, helping stabilize blood sugar levels.

✱ **storing and serving** Toxic if eaten raw but perfectly safe when cooked, yams can generally be substituted in recipes that call for sweet potatoes. Their tough skins are easier to remove after cooking, but wash and peel before mashing or roasting.

yam mash

1 Peel and roughly chop **3 large (1½ pounds) yams.** Cook in boiling water for 20–30 minutes, or until soft.

2 Meanwhile, briefly dry-fry then roughly crush **1 teaspoon each of cumin seeds and coriander seeds.**

3 Drain the yams and mash with the crushed cumin and coriander, **3 tablespoons olive oil, and 4 tablespoons plain yogurt (or crème fraîche).** Season with **salt and pepper,** then serve. **serves 4**

sweet potatoes

The sweet potato is a different species from the yam, with which it is often confused. Sweet potatoes are **packed with carotenoids,** including zeaxanthin, the vision-protecting lutein, and as well as beta-carotene (vitamin A) and vitamin C, which both have antioxidant and **anti-inflammatory** properties. Sweet potatoes are, therefore, good for fighting the free radicals responsible for clogged arteries, heart disease, stroke, cancer and age-related eye diseases. They help reduce inflammation in asthma and rheumatoid arthritis.

Another antioxidant in sweet potatoes is **vitamin E,** which is good for the skin and can soothe skin conditions, such as eczema.

Loaded with starchy carbohydrates and fiber, sweet potatoes release their sugars slowly into the bloodstream, providing long-lasting energy, and they can help stabilize blood sugar levels.

✱ **storing and serving** Store sweet potatoes for several days in a cool, dark, airy place. Do not keep them in the refrigerator. Eat the skins if they are organic. Bake, steam, boil, or roast them.

baked sweet potatoes with salsa

1 Scrub **2 (1½ pounds) sweet potatoes,** and put them in a roasting pan. Prick with a fork and drizzle with **1 tablespoon olive oil** and a little **salt.** Bake in a preheated oven set to 400°F, for 45 minutes.

2 Chop **2 large tomatoes,** ½ **small red onion,** and **1 celery stick,** and mix with a **small handful of chopped fresh cilantro, 2 tablespoons lime juice,** and **2 teaspoons caster sugar.**

3 Halve the sweet potatoes and sprinkle with ½ **cup grated Swiss cheese** and serve topped with the salsa. **serves 2**

NUTRITIONAL CONTENT PER 100 G RAW, YELLOW FLESH: energy 87 calories | **protein** 1 g | **carbohydrates** 21 g | **fat** 0 g | **fiber** 2 g | **vitamin C** 23 mg | **carotene** 3930 mcg | **vitamin E** 4.56 mg

129

pumpkins and butternut squashes

Sharing a similar flavor and texture, pumpkins and butternut squashes are different types of winter squash. Their superb carotenoid content includes lutein and zeaxanthin, which **help protect vision;** and beta-cryptoxanthin, which has been shown to protect against lung and prostate cancers and improve joint health.

Beta-carotene has powerful antioxidant and **anti-inflammatory** properties, so eating pumpkins and butternut squashes can help prevent the clogged arteries that lead to strokes and heart attacks. It may also help reduce the risk of bowel cancer and alleviate inflammatory conditions, such as rheumatoid arthritis.

Both pumpkins and butternut squashes have plenty of fiber, which helps the digestive system function smoothly, especially in people suffering from **irritable bowel syndrome (IBS).**

✽ storing and serving Uncut winter squashes will keep well in a cool, dry place for several months. Bake or roast them for use in hearty stews, or puree for soups. Pumpkins make a delicious pie filling.

roasted pumpkin with walnut and arugula pesto

1 Cut a **2-pound pumpkin** into 8 wedges and discard the seeds. Brush with **olive oil,** season with **salt and pepper,** and roast in a preheated oven set to 425°F, for 20–25 minutes, turning halfway through.

2 Trim and chop **2 scallions** and crush **1 large garlic clove.** Blend with ½ **cup toasted walnuts** and **2 cups arugula** until finely chopped. Blend in **3 tablespoons walnut oil,** and **3 tablespoons olive oil.** Season with **salt and pepper. serves 4**

NUTRITIONAL CONTENT PER 100 G RAW PUMPKIN (BUTTERNUT): energy 13 (36) calories | **protein** 1 (1) g | **carbohydrates** 2 (8) g | **fat** 0 (0) g | **fiber** 1 (2) g | **carotene** 450 (3630) mcg

131

NUTRITIONAL CONTENT PER 100 G RAW: energy 26 calories | protein 2 g | carbohydrates 4 g | fat 0 g | fiber 3 g | vitamin C 49 mg | carotene 385 mcg | vitamin E 0.2 mg | potassium 270 mg

cabbage

All types of cabbage (red, green, and white) are highly nutritious and rich in cancer-fighting glucosinolates—green cabbage has especially high levels. These phytochemicals, including sulforaphane and indoles, **inhibit the growth of tumors** and appear to protect against bowel, ovarian and breast cancers.

Raw cabbage is great for detoxifying the digestive system, soothing indigestion and the aftereffects of stomach upsets, and it helps treat constipation.

Cabbage contains high levels of the antioxidant vitamins A, C, and E, so it helps protect against free-radical damage. The vitamin C content helps to build up resistance to coughs, colds, and other infections.

Pak choi (bok choy) and Savoy cabbage are richer in nutrients than other green and white cabbages. Red cabbage contains the most antioxidants. The vivid color is due to anthocyanidins, potent antioxidants with **anticancer, antimicrobial,** and **anti-inflammatory** properties.

✱ **storing and serving** Store whole cabbages in a cool, dry place for several days. Once cut, cover tightly with plastic wrap, keep in the refrigerator, and use within a day or so. Use cabbage raw in juices or salads. Steam or stir-fry to retain more nutrients.

stir-fried Chinese cabbage

1 Cut **8–10 large Chinese cabbage leaves** diagonally into thin strips.

2 Drain and slice ½ **cup (4 ounces) canned bamboo shoots,** slice **1 onion** and **1 celery stick,** and fry gently in **2 tablespoons vegetable oil** for about 8 minutes, stirring frequently.

3 Add a little **lemon juice** and season with **salt and pepper** to taste. Serve garnished with **lemon slices. serves 4**

133

watercress

The distinctive, peppery taste of watercress has made it a popular garnish, but you should use it for more than livening up a dull salad to make the most of its health-boosting properties. Watercress is a **powerful detoxifier** and contains the antioxidants beta-carotene (vitamin A) and vitamins C and E and **zinc.** These fortify the **immune system** and reduce the risk of heart disease, strokes, and some cancers.

Watercress contains beneficial isothiocyanates, which protect against a known tobacco-borne carcinogen and, therefore, help reduce the risk of lung cancer in smokers.

Eating watercress can help to **reduce blood cholesterol** levels, and its high **iron** content prevents or reduces anemia.

Watercress is an appetite stimulant so is useful for people with small appetites after illness. It is also mildly diuretic and laxative. It can help dissolve kidney and bladder stones.

✳ storing and serving Watercress is best eaten on the day of purchase. Cut away the coarse stems and use the leaves in salads, sandwiches, and soups.

chilled watercress and pear soup

1 Coarsley chop **2 bunches watercress** and cook in **4 tablespoons butter** for 3 minutes, stirring frequently. Peel, core, and slice **3 pears** and add to the pan with 4¼ **cups vegetable stock,** a **pinch of grated nutmeg,** and **pepper** to taste.

2 Bring to a boil then reduce the heat, cover, and simmer for 15–20 minutes. Process to a smooth puree when cool. Stir in **2 tablespoons lemon juice,** cover tightly with plastic wrap, and refrigerate for at least 3 hours.

3 Fold in ⅔ **cup light cream** and serve. **serves 4–6**

NUTRITIONAL CONTENT PER 100 G: energy 22 calories I **protein** 3 g I **carbohydrates** 0 g I **fat** 1 g I **fiber** 3 g I **vitamin C** 62 mg I **carotene** 2520 mcg I **vitamin E** 1.46 mg I **iron** 2.2 mg I **zinc** 0.7 mg

136

NUTRITIONAL CONTENT PER 100 G: energy 12 calories I protein 1 g I carbohydrates 2 g I fat 0 g I fiber 1 g I vitamin C 17 mg I potassium 240 mg I calcium 19 mg I magnesium 5 mg

radishes

Radishes are believed to have been cultivated in Egypt before 2000 B.C., and from there they spread to China and Japan. Of the many different varieties of radish, the best known are probably the small red, white-fleshed globes. There are, however, many other colors and shapes, including the longer-rooted types available in winter. Skin colors include yellow and black as well as red, and there are even radishes with red flesh.

Radishes are related to the brassicas (a family that includes cabbage, kale, and broccoli) and contain significant quantities of the same sulfurous compounds. By **inhibiting the production of cancerous cells,** these glucosinolates are a major force in protecting against cancer.

The same phytochemicals are good for the digestive system and help relieve indigestion and flatulence. Radishes are great for boosting the **immune system.**

The daikon, or mooli, is an oriental radish with a long white root, often juiced for its properties as a blood cleanser and appetite stimulant.

✳ **storing and serving** Radishes will keep in the refrigerator for a day or two. Common radishes are usually eaten raw. Oriental radishes may also be eaten raw but are more often included in stir-fries or pickles.

fresh ricotta with herb oil and radishes

1 Cut **1½ cups ricotta cheese** into thin wedges and arrange them on a plate. Combine **¼ cup olive oil** and **1 tablespoon chopped herbs** (such as basil, chives, mint, or parsley), season with **salt and pepper,** and drizzle over the ricotta.

2 Wash and trim a **bunch of radishes** and arrange around the edge of the plate. Serve with crusty bread. **serves 4**

lettuce

In ancient Egypt, lettuce was sacred to Min, the god of male fertility, but now herbal remedies containing lettuce are **recommended for insomnia.**

Although lettuce consists of 95 percent water, it is still nutritious. The darker the leaves, the more nutrients they contain, and for this reason romaine (or cos) and red-leaved lettuce is far more health-boosting than the pale iceberg types. The darker lettuce is great for eye health, thanks to the antioxidant carotenoids lutein and zeaxanthin, which filter the high-energy light waves responsible for free-radical damage to the eyes. It may, therefore, help reduce the risk of age-related macular degeneration.

Like all leafy greens, lettuce is an important food for women trying to conceive or in the early stages of pregnancy, thanks to its **folate.**

✱ **storing and serving** Uniquely among vegetables, lettuce is available only in its fresh state. Store them in the refrigerator and eat as soon as possible after purchase. Firm lettuce, such as romaine and iceberg, will last longer than soft-leaved lettuce. Lettuce can be braised or included in soups.

smoked chicken and avocado salad

1 Cut **1 pound smoked chicken breast** into bite-size pieces and place them in a large bowl. Add the leaves from **3 romaine lettuce hearts.** Peel, pit, and slice **1 large ripe avocado** and add to the bowl with ¼ **cup grated Parmesan cheese.** Toss well and serve at once. **serves 4**

NUTRITIONAL CONTENT PER 100 G ROMAINE: energy 16 calories I **protein** 1 g I carbohydrates 2 g I **fat** 1 g I **fibre** 1 g I **vitamin C** 5 mg I **carotene** 290 mcg I **folate** 55 mcg

139

NUTRITIONAL CONTENT PER 100 G RAW: energy 33 calories I protein 3 g I carbohydrates 1 g I fat 2 g I fiber 3 g I vitamin C 110 mg I carotene 3145 mcg I vitamin E 1.7 mg I calcium 130 mg

kale

A leafy green vegetable from the brassica family, kale is possibly the closest modern vegetable to a wild cabbage, but the thick-stemmed leaves do not form a head. Kale has the same **cancer-protective sulfurous phytochemicals** as cabbage. These stimulate the body to produce cancer-fighting enzymes and inhibit tumor growth, and they also appear to protect against bowel, ovarian, and breast cancers.

Kale is a really good source of the antioxidant vitamins A, C, and E, which protect against heart disease and cancer and **strengthen the immune system.** Lutein and zeaxanthin are two carotenoids found in kale, which **protect the eyes** from ultraviolet light and help prevent problems, such as cataracts.

Perhaps surprisingly, kale has more available **calcium** than cow's milk. Calcium is essential for healthy bones, so kale is a good choice for those who want the calcium without the calories or who are allergic to dairy products.

✱ **storing and serving** Store kale in the refrigerator and use it quickly because it becomes more bitter as time passes. Kale is usually steamed or stir-fried, although young leaves can be used raw in salads and in juices.

colcannon

1 Shred and remove the stalks of **1 pound kale** and cook for 10 minutes. Boil **5–6 medium (1 pound) unpeeled potatoes** in another pan until tender.

2 Meanwhile, finely chop **6 scallions** and gently simmer in **⅔ cup milk** for 5 minutes.

3 Drain, peel, and mash the potatoes. Add the hot milk and beat well. Drain the kale and beat into the potato with **4 tablespoons butter.** Season with **salt and pepper.** Heat through and serve with extra butter. **serves 4–6**

beets

Beets are closely related to mangelwurzels and sugar beet. It contains high levels of beta-carotene and vitamin C, which help fight off infection and diseases.

Beets also contain **vitamin B$_6$, folate, calcium, iron,** manganese, magnesium, phosphorus, and potassium, which help improve the functioning of the kidneys, gall bladder, and liver and help the body to develop healthy bones, teeth, and muscles. Don't eat too many beets if you have kidney stones, however, because the high levels of oxalates in the vegetable block the body's absorption of **calcium** and iron.

The iron and folate in beets help build up red blood cells, **preventing fatigue and anemia.** Folate also has a role in preventing heart disease and cancer. The iron and manganese in beets help to alleviate particularly low hemoglobin levels caused by very heavy periods and menopausal problems.

✱ **storing and serving** Raw, freshly cooked and canned beetroot contain more nutrients than pickled beets. Beets can also be used in soups, notably the Russian and Polish favorite borsch.

beet and sugar snap pasta

1 Cook **8 ounces pasta** according to the package instructions.

2 Meanwhile, peel and chop **2 medium (8 ounces) cooked beets**. Trim **¾ cup sugar snap peas,** cut them into thirds, and blanch in boiling water for 1 minute.

3 Drain the pasta, return it to the pan, and add the beets and peas. Stir over a low heat for 2 minutes.

4 Remove from the heat. and stir in **1 cup crème fraîche or plain yogurt, 2 tablespoons chopped fresh chives, salt, and pepper.** Serve topped with **grated Parmesan cheese. serves 4**

NUTRITIONAL CONTENT PER 100 G RAW: energy 36 calories l **protein** 2 g l **carbohydrates** 8 g l **fat** 0 g l **fiber** 3 g l **vitamin C** 5 mg l **potassium** 380 mg l **calcium** 20 mg l **magnesium** 11 mg

143

potatoes

A source of filling starchy carbohydrates, potatoes are a great energizing and low-fat food. Eating endless supplies of potato chips and french fries will not give you the benefit of their health-boosting properties!

Potatoes are a good source of **potassium,** which helps reduce high blood pressure. The fiber, especially in the skins, is great for **reducing blood cholesterol levels** and maintaining a healthy digestive system. They also contain vitamin C, which **boosts the immune system,** and cell-building vitamin B_6.

Anyone with depression should eat plenty of potatoes because they are thought to boost production of the brain chemical serotonin, which helps improve mood.

Potatoes may also reduce the risk of bowel and liver cancers, thanks to a phytonutrient called chlorogenic acid, which may inhibit the formation of some carcinogens.

✱ **storing and serving** Some types of potato are better than others for the different methods of cooking. Check labeling for the best cooking methods. Store potatoes in a cool, dark, airy place but not in the refrigerator. Leave them unpeeled if possible to benefit from the most nutrients.

roasted paprika potato wedges

1 Scrub **4 baking potatoes,** 8 ounces each, and cut each lengthways into 8 wedges.

2 Place in a roasting pan, drizzle with **4 tablespoons olive oil,** and toss well to coat. Sprinkle with **1–2 teaspoons paprika** and season with **salt.**

3 Cook in a preheated oven set to 425°F, for 35–40 minutes, basting with the oil 2–3 times during cooking, until the wedges are tender and nicely browned.

4 Serve as a side dish or as a starter with sour cream, aïoli or mayonnaise. **serves 4**

NUTRITIONAL CONTENT PER 100 G, WHOLE BAKED: energy 136 calories | **protein** 4 g | **carbohydrates** 32 g | **fat** 0.2 g | **fiber** 3 g | **vitamin C** 14 mg | **vitamin B_6** 0.54 mg | **potassium** 630 mg

cauliflowers

Some sources say cauliflowers originated in China and were introduced into Spain in the twelfth century. Others say they were an east Mediterranean crop, exported to Italy as recently as the late fifteenth century. Originally, the heads were no larger than tennis balls, but plants with huge heads gradually became popular.

Like other vegetables in the brassica family with the same **cancer-inhibiting sulfurous compounds,** cauliflower has an important role in fighting cancer, especially hormonal, bowel, and lung cancers.

The fiber in cauliflower makes it a heart-protective vegetable because it helps **lower blood cholesterol** levels, and the **folate** helps neutralize excessive levels of heart attack-causing homocysteine.

Cauliflower is a good choice for women before or during early pregnancy because folate can help prevent birth defects, and its vitamin C content is good for **strengthening the immune system.**

✱ **storing and serving** Keep cauliflowers in the refrigerator and use within 1–2 days. Florets can be eaten raw in salads. The briefer the cooking time for cauliflower, the less smelly the sulfurous compounds.

cauliflower relish

1 Cook **2 teaspoons black mustard seeds, and ½ teaspoon each of ground turmeric** and **asafoetida** in **2 tablespoons vegetable oil.**

2 Cut **1 small cauliflower** into bite-size pieces, finely chop **1 red onion,** and deseed and chop **1 fresh green chili.** When the seeds start to pop, add the vegetables and stir-fry for 5 minutes. The cauliflower should be firm to bite.

3 Season to taste with **lemon juice** and **salt** and serve at room temperature. **serves 4**

NUTRITIONAL CONTENT PER 100 G RAW: energy 34 calories | **protein** 4 g | **carbohydrates** 3 g | **fat** 1 g | **fiber** 2 g | **vitamin C** 43 mg | **folate** 66 mcg | **potassium** 380 mg | **calcium** 21 mg

globe artichokes

The edible bud of a type of thistle, globe artichokes may be difficult to eat but are worth the effort. According to researchers at the US Department of Agriculture (USDA), they are the **best vegetable source of antioxidants**—even better than broccoli and spinach.

Globe artichokes have detoxifying qualities and help the liver eliminate toxins from the body more effectively, which helps improve the skin. A phytonutrient called cynarine stimulates the liver's production of bile, which aids digestion and may even help alleviate irritable bowel syndrome (IBS). They are good for heart health, too, because cynarine can also help **lower blood cholesterol** levels and reduce blood pressure.

The **folate** in globe artichokes makes them a good choice for pregnant women or those trying to conceive.

✳ **storing and serving** Fresh globe artichokes will keep for only a few days in the refrigerator. Remove the inedible tips of the leaves and twist off the stalk before cooking and serving with butter or mayonnaise. Ready-to-eat artichoke hearts are available frozen or in cans or jars. Serve these as antipasti or in salads or stir-fries.

artichoke and dill soup

1 Chop **1 onion, 1 garlic clove** and **1 celery stick.** Cook for 10 minutes in **4 tablespoons butter** .

2 Drain and add a **14-ounce can artichoke hearts,** cover, and cook for about 3 minutes. Stir in **4¼ cups vegetable stock, 1 tablespoon lemon juice,** and **1 tablespoon chopped dill** and cook, covered, for 15 minutes. Puree the soup in batches, transfer to a saucepan, and reheat gently.

3 Mix **12 tablespoons all-purpose flour** with **⅔ cup vegetable stock.** Stir into the soup. Add **2 tablespoons chopped dill,** season with **salt and pepper,** then stir in **⅔ cup light cream. serves 4**

NUTRITIONAL CONTENT PER 100 G COOKED: energy 8 calories | protein 1 g | carbohydrates 1 g | fat 0 g | fiber 0 g | folate 21 mcg | potassium 140 mg | calcium 19 mg

149

NUTRITIONAL CONTENT PER 100 G RAW: energy 42 calories | protein 4 g | carbohydrates 4 g | fat 1 g | fiber 4 g | vitamin C 215 mg | folate 135 mcg | vitamin E 1 mg | potassium 450 mg

brussels sprouts

Resembling miniature cabbages, brussels sprouts are one of the top brassicas (a group including broccoli, kale, cabbage, and cauliflower) for their content of **cancer-fighting phytonutrients.** These work by neutralizing and then removing cancer-causing substances from the body and by deactivating the estrogens responsible for hormone-related cancers. Sprouts are, therefore, particularly good for preventing digestive and colorectal cancers, and ovarian and breast cancers.

Brussels sprouts are a top source of the antioxidants, especially vitamins A and C, that are useful for keeping the body disease free. In addition, the carotenoids lutein and zeaxanthin help to maintain healthy vision.

During early pregnancy sprouts are useful for their **folate**, a vitamin that also helps protect the heart.

The good quantity of fiber in sprouts means they are great for the digestive system and help prevent diseases, such as diverticulosis. The fiber can also help **reduce blood cholesterol** levels.

✳ storing and serving Keep brussels sprouts in the refrigerator for 1–2 days, or they will quickly turn yellow. Boil, braise, microwave, or steam sprouts. Cut a cross into the end of large ones to speed up the cooking process, which should be short to prevent nutrient loss.

Brussels sprouts with chestnuts

1 Trim **3 dozen (1½ pounds) Brussels sprouts** and cook in lightly salted boiling water for 10–12 minutes, or until tender.

2 Meanwhile, drain a **7-ounce can chestnuts** into a saucepan, add enough **vegetable stock** to cover, and heat gently.

3 Drain the sprouts and the chestnuts. Stir the chestnuts into the sprouts with **1 tablespoon butter** and season with **salt and pepper. serves 4–5**

151

chicory and endive

Chicory and endive belong to two closely related botanical families but are different plants. The European chicory is a relatively new crop in the United States. Curly endive is sometimes called chicory, but it is one of three main endive varieties, which also include Belgian endive and escarole.

Chicory and endive encourage the growth of "good" bacteria in the gut, helping to prevent indigestion and disease, and they **improve the body's absorption of nutrients.** They stimulate the appetite, which is good for anyone recovering from illness.

Terpenoids, plant enzymes, help to improve the body's detoxification ability. They also help maintain kidney health and increase urine output.

Both greens are a good source of vitamins A (beta-carotene) and C. They also contain **calcium,** good for helping prevent osteoporosis, and **folate,** excellent during pregnancy.

✱ storing and serving Keep chicory and endive in the refrigerator. Usually served as leafy salad greens, they may be briefly baked, steamed, or sauteed and served as a main or side dish.

endive and avocado salad

1 Tear ½ **head of curly endive** into pieces and put them in a salad bowl with a **bunch of watercress** separated into sprigs.

2 Halve **2 avocados,** remove the pits, and slice the flesh into a bowl. Pour **6 tablespoons French dressing** over the avocados and toss gently until the slices are completely coated.

3 Add the dressed avocado to the endive leaves and toss together. **serves 6**

NUTRITIONAL CONTENT PER 100 G ENDIVE, RAW: energy 13 calories I **protein** 2 g I **carbohydrates** 1 g I **fat** 0 g I **fiber** 2 g I **vitamin C** 12 mg I **carotene** 440 mcg I **potassium** 380 mg

153

honey

A powerful **natural antiseptic** often used for coughs and sore throats, honey also has **antibacterial properties** so is good for stomach upsets.

For those suffering from pollen-triggered hay fever, naturopaths recommend a daily dose of unprocessed organic honey, including honeycomb wax, to build a resistance to pollen. Daily consumption of honey also increases the body's levels of antioxidants, which protect against free-radical-inflicted cellular damage.

Honey is a better sweetener than refined sugar for diabetics because it has less effect on blood sugar levels. It may help **reduce levels of blood cholesterol** and of homocysteine, a risk factor for heart disease.

Use honey in moderation because it is high in calories, and never feed it to babies under one year old because their digestive systems can not process it.

✳ **storing and serving** Raw, unprocessed honey direct from the hive is more nutritious than store bought honey, which has had many of its phyto-nutrients destroyed by heat treatment. Keep honey in a cool, dark place and use it in place of sugar, but halve the quantity required because it is twice as sweet.

honey and yogurt with prune puree

1 Put **20 (8 ounces) ready-to-eat pitted prunes** in a saucepan with the juice and finely grated rind of **1 lemon** and **8 tablespoons cold water.** Cover and simmer for 6–8 minutes, then blend the mix to a coarse puree.

2 Spoon the puree into 4 glasses and add a layer of **2–3 tablespoons clear honey** to each. Divide **2 cups plain yogurt** among the glasses, then sprinkle each with ½ **tablespoon crunchy muesli.** Serve immediately.
serves 4

NUTRITIONAL CONTENT PER 100 G (1 TBSP = 25 G): energy 288 calories I **protein** 0 g I **carbohydrates** 76 g I **fat** 0 g I **fiber** 0 g I **potassium** 35 mg I **calcium** 8 mg I **magnesium** 2 mg

155

NUTRITIONAL CONTENT PER 100 G: energy 266 calories I protein 0 g I carbohydrates 69 g I fat 0 g I fiber 0 g I potassium 1460 mg I calcium 210 mg I magnesium 240 mg I iron 4.7 mg

molasses

A dark, thick, sweet syrup extracted from sugar cane, molasses is packed with all the nutrients missing from refined sugar: B vitamins, **calcium, iron, potassium,** magnesium, and copper. Blackstrap molasses is the most nutritious type. Its bittersweet flavor varies greatly according to brand, so experiment until you find one you like that has not been processed with sulfur.

Molasses is an iron-rich food—one tablespoon contains more than three times the iron found in an egg—so it is great for building red blood cells, increasing energy, and preventing fatigue and anemia. A tablespoon of molasses also contains more calcium than a glass of milk and more potassium than almost any other food. Molasses is, therefore, great for bone health and preventing osteoporosis.

Molasses keeps skin and hair looking healthy, and a recent study from Harvard-affiliated McLean Hospital suggests a compound called uridine, found in molasses, may be helpful for preventing depression.

✱ **storing and serving** Store molasses, tightly sealed, at room temperature or in the refrigerator for up to six months. Try adding to soups, baked beans, meat stews, gingerbread, or milk.

fig and molasses cake bars

1 Beat together ½ **cup (1 stick) unsalted butter,** ¼ **cup sugar,** and **3 tablespoons molasses.** Slowly add **3 beaten eggs.**

2 Add ½ **cup roughly chopped hazelnuts, 1 teaspoon vanilla extract,** 1½ **cups all-purpose flour, 1 teaspoon baking powder,** and ½ **teaspoon ground cinnamon** and mix thoroughly.

3 Stir in **10 medium dried figs,** chopped. Spoon the mixture into a greased and lined 7- x 11- inch cake pan and bake in a preheated oven set to 350°F, for 20 minutes. Cut into bars. **makes 14**

NUTRITIONAL CONTENT PER 100 G PITTED IN JUICE: energy 103 calories | **protein** 1 g | **carbohydrates** 0 g | **fat** 11 g | **fiber** 4 g | **potassium** 91 mg | **calcium** 61 mg | **magnesium** 22 mg

olives and olive oil

The low incidence of serious disease among and longevity of Mediterranean populations is attributed to certain key foods, among them olives and olive oil, which is made from crushed and pressed olives.

The health-boosting properties of olives and olive oil are due to the **"good" monounsaturated fatty acids** and many antioxidants. Eating a small handful of olives a day or using olive oil in place of other fats is highly protective toward the heart, thanks to the various compounds that help **reduce blood cholesterol** levels and blood pressure and prevent blood clots.

The specific monounsaturated fats in olives and olive oil are thought to help protect against cancer, particularly breast cancer, and phenols are believed to protect against bowel cancer.

The monounsaturates in olive oil may also help relieve inflammatory conditions, including rheumatoid arthritis and asthma, and help maintain the memory areas of the brain.

✱ **storing and serving** Store both olives and olive oil away from heat and light. Olives can be served as a snack or used to flavor pizzas, pasta sauces, or salads. Use virgin olive oil for cooking and extra virgin for drizzling and for salad dressings.

sweet oat cakes

1 Mix together **3⅓ cups rolled oats,** ⅓ **cup sesame seeds, 3 tablespoons poppy seeds,** and a **pinch of salt.** Pour in ½ **cup boiling water, 2 tablespoons clear honey,** and **7 tablespoons olive oil** and stir to form a soft dough.

2 Shape the dough into 20 balls the size of a walnut. Place them on nonstick parchment paper and flatten them with the palm of your hand to make 3½-inch rounds. Bake in a preheated oven set to, 350°F, for about 15 minutes, until golden.

3 Let cool on a wire rack and serve with a wedge of cheese and a bunch of grapes. **makes 20**

NUTRITIONAL CONTENT PER 100 G SOFT, STEAMED: energy 73 calories I **protein** 8 g I **carbohydrates** 1 g I **fat** 4 g I **fiber** 0 g I **vitamin E** 0.95 mg I **folate** 15 mcg I **calcium** 510 mg I **iron** 1.2 mg

soy and tofu

Although soy has been a major food plant in the Far East for thousands of years, it has become important in the West in only the last few decades. The main soy-based product is tofu (bean curd), made from the "milk" of crushed soy beans. Soy milk is useful for those allergic to dairy products, and soy sauce, made from fermented soy beans, is essential in oriental cuisine.

Soy offers protection against cancer, heart disease, and osteoporosis. This is due mainly to the protein and fiber content, which **lowers blood cholesterol levels** and keeps the digestive system healthy, and to the phytoestrogens called isoflavones. These plant hormones seem to protect against hormone-related cancers. Isoflavones can help relieve the symptoms of the menopause and premenstrual syndrome (PMS).

Soy is an excellent source of protein and, unlike most animal proteins, lowers blood pressure and cholesterol levels. Its **omega-3 fatty acids** improve heart muscle function.

✽ **storing and serving** Fresh soy beans are not widely available. Use dried beans soaked and cooked in soups and casseroles or sprout them to make bean sprouts. Use silken tofu in dressings and dips, and soft or firm tofu in cooking and smoothies.

peach and tofu smoothie

1 Roughly chop **6 tablespoons dried peaches** in a blender with **½ cup soft tofu.** Add a little juice from **1¼ cups chilled apple juice** and blend to a smooth puree.

2 Add the remaining apple juice and blend again until frothy. Pour into a tall glass, add ice cubes, and serve. **serves 1–2**

161

milk

Although it contains high-quality protein, cow's milk is best known for its **calcium** content. Working together with the phosphorous and vitamins D and K in milk, calcium promotes the development of strong bones and teeth. An iron-binding protein in milk, lactoferrin, can help prevent and even reverse osteoporosis.

Young children need whole milk for development, but adults are advised to consume milk with a reduced-fat content. Such milk actually has more calcium than whole milk.

Cow's milk supports healthy thyroid function, thanks to its **iodine** content, and studies have revealed that it helps reduce the risk of gout.

A calcium-rich diet is associated with fat loss so slimmers may benefit from an increased intake of low-fat dairy foods while following a reduced-calorie diet.

People who are allergic to cow's milk often tolerate **goat's milk.** It offers the same main health benefits as cow's milk.

✱ **storing and serving** Milk should be kept in the refrigerator and used within a few days of opening.

milk junket with rhubarb

1 Gently heat **1 vanilla pod** in **2½ cups milk** until warm. Stir in **1 tablespoon sugar.**

2 Remove from the heat. Scrape out the vanilla pod seeds and add them to the milk. Stir **10 drops rennet** into the milk, and pour the mixture into a large bowl. Let cool and place in the refrigerator to set.

3 Roughly chop **6–12 stalks (1½ pounds) rhubarb** and cook with the juice and grated rind of **1 orange.** Add **2 tablespoons sugar** and cook for 6–8 minutes, until the rhubarb has softened. Let cool and serve with a spoonful of the milk junket and **toasted almonds. serves 4–6**

NUTRITIONAL CONTENT PER 100 ML SEMI-SKIMMED: energy 46 calories | protein 3 g | carbohydrates 5 g | fat 2 g | fiber 0 g | vitamin C 1 mg | potassium 150 mg | calcium 120 mg

live yogurt

Yogurt is made by adding bacterial cultures to milk. It contains plenty of nutrients, including **calcium,** but is revered for its live bacteria. Look for "live and active bacteria" on labels. The bacteria in live yogurt, *Lactobacillus bulgaricus* and *Streptoccus thermophilus,* together with other probiotics, support the friendly bacteria in the intestine. A daily helping of yogurt helps **protect the digestive system** and fight against gastroenteritis, diarrhea and food poisoning.

Live yogurt is useful for restoring the bacterial balance in the gut after taking conventional antibiotics. It can help prevent and treat ulcers caused by the *Helicobater pylori* bacterium. It can also help counter yeast infections and help reduce bad breath and keep the mouth healthy.

The calcium in yogurt is good for healthy bones and teeth. The beneficial bacteria in yogurt is killed by pasteurization so organic yogurt is the best choice.

✱ storing and serving Use yogurt in dips, dressings, and sauces, in cooking, cake mixtures, smoothies, and as a topping instead of cream.

blueberry and blackberry yogurt syllabub

1 Gently heat ¾ **cup blackberries** for 2–3 minutes, until the juice begins to run out. Remove from the heat and stir in ½ **cup blueberries**.

2 Whisk ⅔ **cup heavy cream** with **1–2 tablespoons clear honey** until softly peaking, then stir in **1 tablespoon orange liqueur**. Fold in **1¼ cups pint) plain yogurt.**

3 Spoon the berries and their juice into 4 bowls and top with the yogurt mixture. Sprinkle over **1 tablespoon toasted flaked almonds** and refrigerate for 1–2 hours before serving. **serves 4**

NUTRITIONAL CONTENT PER 100 G PLAIN LOW-FAT: energy 56 calories | **protein** 5 g | carbohydrates 8 g | **fat** 1 g | **fiber** 0 g | **potassium** 250 mg | **calcium** 190 mg | **magnesium** 19 mg

NUTRITIONAL CONTENT PER MEDIUM EGG: calories 76 calories | **protein** 6 g |
carbohydrates 0 g | **fat** 5 g | **fiber** 0 g | **potassium 65 mg** | **calcium** 29 g | **magnesium** 6 g

eggs

Eating high-cholesterol foods such as eggs was once thought to raise cholesterol levels in the body. It is now known that it is the foods that are high in saturated fat, meats, pastry, and high-fat cheese, for example, rather than dietary cholesterol that raise blood cholesterol levels and increase the risk of heart attacks. Indeed, eating eggs may offer some protection against heart disease, breast cancer, and eye problems.

One study suggests that eating an egg each day may give teenage girls additional protection against breast cancer in later life, thanks to the presence of amino acids, B vitamins, vitamins A, D, and E, **iodine, selenium, phosphorus,** and two **vision-protecting carotenoids,** lutein and zeaxanthin.

Pregnant and nursing women, young children, and the elderly should avoid eating undercooked or raw eggs (found in homemade mayonnaise and uncooked desserts, such as mousses) because of the risk of food poisoning from salmonella. Pasteurized eggs are the safest option, because pasteurizing kills the bacteria.

✻ **storing and serving** Eat eggs before their 'expiration date' date. Salmonella bacteria multiply with age, so the fresher the egg the better. An excellent source of protein, eggs are ideal for any meal.

watercress and mushroom frittata

1 Sautee **2¾ cups sliced mushrooms** in **3 tablespoons butter,** stirring occasionally, for 3 minutes.

2 Meanwhile, combine **6 beaten eggs** with **5 tablespoons grated Parmesan cheese,** a **bunch of watercress** (tough stems removed) and plenty of **pepper.** Add to the mushrooms and mix gently.

3 Reduce the heat and cook until the egg mixture is slightly set and the underside golden. Place the pan under a preheated moderate broiler to cook the top of the frittata. **serves 3–4**

167

walnuts

Walnut trees were first domesticated thousands of years ago in northern Iran and Turkey, but today the largest commercial producer of walnuts is California. Walnuts are great for heart health, being excellent sources of monounsaturated fats, omega-6 fats, and, unusually, of the **omega-3 fatty acids** found mostly in oily fish. These unsaturated fats help **lower cholesterol levels,** prevent blood clotting and reduce the risk of sudden death from dangerous, abnormal heart rhythms.

The omega-3 fats in walnuts, which affect levels of the mood-altering brain chemical serotonin, make them useful for dealing with depression. They also contain melatonin, which aids the body's natural sleep patterns, so they may help deal with insomnia.

Walnuts are good for boosting energy levels, but be aware that they are highly calorific if you need to watch your weight.

✷ storing and serving The oils in nuts makes them go stale quickly, so always check the 'expiration' dates on packaged walnuts and choose fresh walnuts in their shells where possible. Use walnuts raw as a snack, in breakfast cereals, salads, cakes, and breads.

walnut and sunflower seed snacks

1 Mix together **4 tablespoons sunflower seeds** and **3 tablespoons sesame seeds,** spread over a baking sheet, and toast under a preheated broiler for 2–3 minutes.

2 Mix with **1¾ cups roughly chopped walnuts** and **1 tablespoon raisins.** While the seeds are still warm, mix in **3 tablespoons honey.** Divide the mixture into walnut-sized portions and, with damp hands, firmly press into balls.

3 Place the balls on parchment paper. Let cool and dry for 3–4 hours or overnight. **makes 24**

NUTRITIONAL CONTENT PER 100 G (NO SHELLS:) energy 688 calories I **protein** 15 g I **carbohydrates** 3 g I **fat** 69 g I **fiber** 6 g I **vitamin E** 3.83 mg I **potassium** 450 mg I **magnesium** 160 mg

Brazil nuts

Brazil nuts are very high in fat (although most of this is the "good," unsaturated kind) and so should be eaten sparingly. However, they are by far the best food source of the antioxidant **selenium.** A trace mineral, selenium protects the body against free radicals and has an **anticancer** function.

Because of their selenium content, Brazil nuts may also be useful in protecting against prostate problems, which commonly affect men from the age of 40 and upward. In addition, eating Brazil nuts may raise spirits as selenium affects mood, and low selenium levels can lead to irritability, depression, and fatigue.

These nuts are a good source of protein for vegetarians and vegans because, weight for weight, they contain as much protein as eggs.

✱ **storing and serving** Keep unshelled nuts in a cool place for no more than a couple of months. Shelled nuts should be transferred to a sealed container in the refrigerator to prevent them from going stale. Use raw as a snack or mixed with breakfast cereal or cook them in a range of dishes.

Chickpea cakes

1 Chop ⅔ **cups Brazil nuts.** Drain **2 14-ounce cans organic chickpeas.** Blend nuts and chickpeas until smooth. Chop **1 small onion** and mix with ¼ **cup sunflower seeds** and **1 tablespoon chopped parsley.**

2 Beat **1 egg** with **salt and pepper,** combine with chickpea mixture, and blend together. Using a large tablespoon, press the mixture into 8 or 16 flat patties.

3 Dip each patty in **lightly beaten egg** and coat with **1 cup dried whole-meal bread-crumbs.** Chill for 4 hours or overnight, then shallow-fry in **vegetable oil** until golden-brown. Serve with a tomato sauce and vegetables. **serves 4**

NUTRITIONAL CONTENT PER 100 G (WHOLE:) energy 682 calories | **protein** 14 g | **carbohydrates** 3 g | **fat** 68 g | **fiber** 8 g | **vitamin E** 7.18 mg | **selinium** 1530 mcg | **potassium** 660 mg

171

hazelnuts

Hazelnuts, also known as filberts and cobnuts, are one of the richest dietary sources of **vitamin E.** This powerful antioxidant helps neutralize free radicals, which are responsible for cell destruction and disease. It is also essential for healthy muscles and supports the body's red blood cells, preventing anemia.

Hazelnuts are a good source of manganese, which plays a role in blood sugar regulation and may help reduce symptoms of premenstrual stress (PMS), and the anti-oxidant **zinc,** which, eaten regularly, can offer protection against cancer, heart disease, and premature ageing.

Other heart-protective nutrients in hazelnuts include omega-6 oils, plant sterols, and fiber, all of which help **lower blood cholesterol** levels. Because they are a rich source of fiber, hazelnuts are good for the digestive system. The fiber helps the digestive tract function smoothly, reducing the risk of bowel cancer.

✱ **storing and serving** For maximum nutrients and flavor buy unprocessed hazelnuts. Shell and eat as they are or roast gently to release more flavor. Eat as a snack, add to salads, or use in cakes and cookies.

grapefruit and shrimp salad

1 Halve **2 large pink grapefruit** and loosen the segments, but leave them in the skins.

2 Sprinkle a **pinch of chili flakes, 1 teaspoon honey,** and a **pinch of paprika** over the segments and broil for 5–6 minutes. Spoon out the grapefruit segments and add to a bowl with **8 ounces cooked peeled shrimp, 1 cup bean sprouts,** and **1 tablespoon chopped fresh cilantro.** Dry-fry ¾ **cup hazelnuts,** chop, and mix in the bowl.

3 Mix **2 tablespoons lemon juice, 1 tablespoon olive oil, 1 teaspoon honey, salt, and pepper,** pour over the salad, and toss. **serves 4**

NUTRITIONAL CONTENT PER 100 G SHELLED NUTS: energy 650 calories | protein 14 g | carbohydrates 6 g | fat 64 g | fiber 9 g | vitamin E 25 mg | zinc 2.2 mg | manganese 4.9 mg

173

NUTRITIONAL CONTENT PER 100 G ROASTED, SALTED CASHEWS: energy

611 calories | **protein** 21 g | **carbohydrates** 19 g | **fat** 51 g | **fiber** 3 g | **iron** 6.2 mg | **copperl** 2.04 mg

cashews

If you are prone to anemia and fatigue, eating cashews regularly—for both their **copper and iron** content—will help build the red blood cells your body needs. They contain roughly twice as much iron as almonds, walnuts, and hazelnuts. Eat them with a vitamin C-rich fruit or fruit juice to increase your body's absorption of the iron.

The high levels of magnesium in cashews are important for strengthening bones, hair, and teeth. They are a good source of the mineral **zinc,** which is essential for healthy skin, hair, and nails, healing wounds, and improving immunity. In addition, they contain beta-carotene, which the body converts to vitamin A, an antioxidant vitamin essential for immune health and building resistance to disease.

Like all nuts, cashews are a good source of protein for vegetarians.

✳ storing and serving Cashews are always sold shelled because the shells contain an oily liquid that can cause the skin to blister. Keep them in the refrigerator for up to six months. If you eat cashews as a snack, avoid too many salted ones, especially if you have high blood pressure. Add raw cashews to breakfast cereal or use them in salads or stir-fries.

cashew chicken

1 Heat **1 cup chicken stock** in a saucepan. Cube and add **13 ounces chicken breast** and bring to a boil. Simmer for 5 minutes. Remove chicken and set aside.

2 Add **2 tablespoons yellow bean sauce.** Cook for a couple of minutes. Slice and add **3 medium carrots** and **7 ounces bamboo shoots.** Cook for another couple of minutes.

3 Return the chicken to the pan, bring the sauce to a boil, and thicken with **1 teaspoon corn starch** mixed with **2 tablespoons water.**

4 Stir in **1½ cups cashew nuts** and **1 shredded scallion** before serving with boiled white rice. **serves 2**

175

almonds

One of the earliest nut trees to be cultivated, almonds were being grown in the Mediterranean by 3000 B.C.

These nuts are rich in the monounsaturated fats that help protect against heart disease by **lowering blood cholesterol levels.** Almond skins contain flavonoids, which work in tandem with almonds' antioxidant **vitamin E** and can help prevent clogged arteries.

Vitamin E is also protective against cancer, as are two phytochemicals found in almonds, quercetin and kaempferol, which can suppress tumor growth.

Weight for weight, almonds are richer in protein than eggs, so they are a good choice for vegetarians. Their protein does need "completing" with legumes.

Almonds are also particularly high in **calcium**— 2 ounces of almonds contain more calcium than half a cup of milk—which the body needs for strengthening bones and teeth. Almonds can, therefore, be a good for people who are intolerant of dairy products.

✱ storing and serving Almonds are most nutritious when eaten raw and unsalted. The oils in nuts give them a limited shelf life and they can become rancid easily. If possible, buy them in their shells.

almond macaroons

1 Mix together ¾ **cup ground almonds** and ½ **cup plus 2 tablespoons sugar.** Whisk together ½ **teaspoon almond extract** and **2 large egg whites** until stiff. Fold in the ground almond mixture.

2 Place teaspoonfuls of the mixture on lined baking sheets, leaving spaces between them so they can expand slightly. Cook in a preheated oven set to 350°F, for 15 minutes, until slightly firm.

3 Remove the macaroons from the oven and let cool for 5 minutes. Lift them off the parchment paper with a rubber spatula and let cool completely. **makes about 16**

NUTRITIONAL CONTENT PER 100 G (NO SHELLS:) energy 612 calories | **protein** 21 g | **carbohydrates** 7 g | **fat** 56 g | **fiber** 13 g | **vitamin E** 24 mg | **potassium** 870 mg | **calcium** 240 mg

oats

Countless studies have shown that a daily helping of oats is **heart protective** because the soluble fiber in oats sticks to "bad" cholesterol and removes it from the body, thereby preventing it from clogging arteries.

Oats are a particularly good food at the start of the day because their fiber content ensures that sugars are released slowly into the bloodstream, providing energy without upsetting blood sugar levels.

In addition, eating oats reduces the risk of cancer because of the presence of a trace mineral in oats called **selenium**, plant hormones called lignans, and the insoluble fiber they contain. Selenium is linked with a reduced risk of bowel and prostate cancers, lignans account for a lowered risk of hormone-related cancers, and the insoluble fiber attacks certain bile acids, making them less toxic and potentially carcinogenic. Selenium may also help ward off depression.

✻ **storing and serving** Oats will keep for a couple of months in an airtight container. Enjoy them raw in muesli or cooked in porridge. They make an ideal coating for fried fish or a crumble topping, or use them for baking muesli bars, or cookies.

blueberry porridge and nuts

1 Gently heat ½ **cup blueberries** and **1–3 tablespoons sugar** (to taste) for 6 minutes, or until the berry juice begins to run. Remove from heat.

2 Put **2 cups rolled oats** and **4¼ cups milk** in a pan. Add **sugar** to taste and bring to a boil, stirring constantly. Simmer for 6–8 minutes, stirring from time to time, and add extra milk if you want.

3 Serve the porridge topped with blueberries, **3 tablespoons toasted nuts**, a little **soft dark brown sugar**, and **1–2 tablespoons toasted wheat germ.** Pour some **buttermilk (or yogurt)** over the porridge and serve. **serves 4**

NUTRITIONAL CONTENT PER 100 G ROLLED, RAW: energy 400 calories | **protein** 12 g | **carbohydrates** 73 g | **fat** 9 g | **fiber** 6 g | **potassium** 370 mg | **magnesium** 110 mg | **selenium** 3 mcg

sunflower seeds

Because they contain the goodness necessary to germinate a new plant, all seeds are a concentrated source of nutrients. Sunflower seeds (they are technically a fruit, known as achenes) are particularly health-boosting for their rich **vitamin E** content, and their **selenium** and magnesium.

The antioxidant vitamin E and the trace mineral, selenium, work especially well together to **protect against cancer.** Sunflower seeds may benefit those with rheumatoid arthritis and asthma because they have **anti-inflammatory** properties.

Sunflower seeds are high in the beneficial and essential unsaturated fats (omega-6). They also contain cholesterol-lowering compounds called phytosterols, vitamin E, which helps disarm free radicals, and magnesium, which helps reduce high blood pressure.

✱ **storing and serving** The fat in sunflower seeds can turn them rancid, so keep them in an airtight container, preferably in the refrigerator. Dry-frying or roasting sunflower seeds enhances their flavor. Snack on them, add them to stir-fries and salads, or use them in home baking.

mixed seed snacks

1 Put **1¾ cups assorted seeds** (including sunflower, pumpkin, hemp, flaxseed/linseed and sesame seeds) into a bowl, add **2 tablespoons tamari sauce,** and stir until all the seeds are covered with the sauce.

2 Drain the seeds through a fine sieve, then dry-fry in a hot pan for a few minutes, until golden-brown. Remove the pan from the heat, lift out the seeds onto a piece of paper towel and let cool.
serves 4

NUTRITIONAL CONTENT PER 100 G RAW: energy 582 calories | **protein** 20 g | **carbohydrates** 19 g | **fat** 48 g | **fiber** 6 g | **vitamin E** 38 mg | **magnesium** 270 mg | **selenium** 49 mcg

pumpkin seeds

Men of middle age and beyond would do well to snack regularly on pumpkin seeds because they are an excellent food for maintaining prostate health and reducing the risk of prostate cancer. This is believed to be due to the high levels of **zinc** and to certain compounds in pumpkin seed oil. Zinc also supports bone mineral density, which is as important for older men as it is for postmenopausal women.

Pumpkin seeds make an energizing snack because of their energy-producing zinc, and iron, which boosts blood cells. They also contribute to a healthy heart, thanks to their essential **omega-3 fatty acids** and **cholesterol-lowering compounds** called phytosterols.

Eating pumpkin seeds may help to lift the spirits because of their zinc, B vitamins, and omega-3 fats, all of which can help prevent depression.

✱ storing and serving Pumpkin seeds are available roasted or raw. Keep them in the refrigerator because of their oil content. Eat as a snack, add to cereals, soups, casseroles, and salads, or use them in home baking. Pumpkin seed oil can be used to dress salads or added to protein drinks.

pumpkin seed dip

1 Dry-fry **1 cup pumpkin seeds** over a moderate heat for 5–10 minutes. Shake the pan and turn them as they pop and become golden brown. Remove the pan from the heat and let cool.

2 Grind the seeds coarsely in a food processor and skin, deseed, and dice **3 large tomatoes.** Add **2 finely chopped garlic cloves, 3–5 chopped scallions**, **½ teaspoon ground cumin,** the juice of ½ **lime,** and **3 tablespoons tomato paste,** and blend until the mixture is smooth. **serves 4**

NUTRITIONAL CONTENT PER 100 G RAW: energy 569 calories I **protein** 24 g I **carbohydrates** 15 g I **fat** 46 g I **fiber** 5 g I **potassium** 820 mg I **magnesium** 270 mg I **zinc** 6.6 mg

183

sesame seeds

Widely used in Middle Eastern cooking, sesame seeds are the main ingredient in tahini, a paste used to make hummus. Of all the nuts and seeds, sesame seeds have the highest content of phytosterols, plant compounds that are believed to **reduce blood cholesterol** levels, **boost the immune system,** and reduce the risk of certain types of cancer.

Sesame seeds are a good source of **calcium,** so a useful alternative for anyone allergic to dairy products. They may also provide some relief from rheumatoid arthritis because of their high levels of copper, which has **anti-inflammatory** properties. The magnesium in sesame seeds relaxes blood vessels and may benefit migraine sufferers.

Cooking with sesame seed oil can lower blood pressure, thanks to an antioxidant called sesamin.

✱ **storing and serving** Once hulled, sesame seeds should be kept in the refrigerator to prevent the oils from turning rancid. Sprinkle over vegetables or salads, or use in home baking.

honeyed granola

1 Warm **3 tablespoons sunflower oil** and **3 tablespoons thick honey** in a sacepan.

2 Stir in **2 tablespoons golden linseeds, 2 tablespoons sesame seeds, ⅓ cup roughly chopped hazelnuts, ½ cup barley flakes, ½ cup rye flakes, ½ cup millet flakes.**

3 Spread the mixture evenly over a lightly oiled baking sheet with edges. Bake in a preheated oven set to 350°F, for 8–10 minutes, stirring the mixture half way through cooking.

3 Let cool, then transfer to a storage jar. Store in a cool place for up to 2 weeks. **serves 6**

NUTRITIONAL CONTENT PER 100 g: energy 598 calories I **protein** 18 g I **carbohydrates** 1 g I **fat** 58 g I **fiber** 8 g I calcium 670 mg I **potassium** 570 mg I **magnesium** 370 mg I **copper** 1.46 mg

flaxseed

Also known as linseed, these are the seeds of the flax plant. The largest plant source of essential **omega-3 fatty acids,** flaxseed is important for vegetarians because the other main dietary source is oily fish. These fats thin the blood and, together with fiber, help **lower blood cholesterol** levels, which explains the role of flaxseed and flaxseed oil in protecting against heart disease.

Flaxseed also **helps combat cancer,** especially breast and bowel cancers. This is due partly to lignans, anti-estrogen plant compounds that are protective against hormone-related cancers, and partly to fiber. This fiber is great for the digestive system, speeding potentially carcinogenic substances out of the body, and it also makes flaxseed a good remedy for constipation and of help to people with irritable bowel syndrome (IBS).

✱ **storing and serving** Flaxseed is available whole or ground, but the nutrients are more easily absorbed when ground. Store whole flaxseed in an airtight container; keep ground flaxseed and flaxseed oil refrigerated. Add ground flaxseed to juices, smoothies, yogurt, cereal, breads, and cookies. Don't heat flaxseed oil—use it in salad dressings or drinks. Industrial blends of linseed oil are not for internal consumption.

flaxseed crackers

1 Sift together **1 cup whole-meal flour, 1 cup all-purpose flour, ½ teaspoon baking powder,** and **½ teaspoon baking soda,** adding any bran left in the sifter or sieve. Stir in **3 tablespoons golden flaxseeds** and a **pinch of salt.** Rub in **4 tablespoons butter** and **3 tablespoons olive oil** and add about **1 tablespoon water** to make a smooth dough.

2 Roll out the dough to about ¼ inch thick. Cut out rounds and transfer to a greased baking sheet. Bake in a preheated oven set to 400°F, for 15 minutes. Cool on a wire rack. **makes about 20**

sardines and mackerel

Oily fish, such as sardines and mackerel, are particularly beneficial due to their **omega-3 fatty acids,** which are vital for brain function and a healthy heart. According to the American Heart Association, eating two portions of oily fish weekly can prevent heart attacks.

Omega-3 fatty acids are also linked with reducing the severity of inflammatory disorders and may be useful for people with asthma, rheumatoid arthritis, and psoriasis.

Sardines and mackerel provide vitamin D, which is important for strong bones and teeth, and **selenium,** an antioxidant mineral linked with a reduced cancer risk.

Unlike canned tuna, canned sardines and mackerel retain their beneficial oils and match the fresh fish for nutritional content. Fish canned with their bones (which soften during the canning process) are rich in **calcium, phosphorus,** and fluoride, so are great for maintaining bone health and preventing osteoporosis.

✱ **storing and serving** Keep fresh fish in the refrigerator or, if it has not been frozen previously, in the freezer. Serve mackerel simply with a squeeze of lemon or team it with tart flavors, such as gooseberry. Sardines are a good fish for the barbecue.

spiced mackerel and celeriac mash

1 Mix **1 teaspoon cumin seeds, 1 teaspoon crushed black peppercorns,** and a **pinch of chili flakes** and sprinkle over **4 mackerel,** gutted and descaled. Cover. Refrigerate for 2–3 hours.

2 Put the mackerel into an ovenproof dish, stuff the cavities with **dill sprigs** and pour ⅔ cup apple juice over the fish. Loosely cover with foil and bake in a preheated oven set to 400°F, for 15–20 minutes.

3 Boil **2 cups peeled and dried celeriac** for 5 minutes. Peel and dice **4–5 medium (1½ pounds) potatoes,** then add for 15 minutes. Drain and mash with **milk** and **olive oil. serves 4**

NUTRITIONAL CONTENT PER 100 G SARDINES (MACKEREL): energy 165 (223) calories I **protein** 21 (19) g I **carbohydrates** 0 (0) g I **fat** 9 (16) g I **fiber** 0 (0) g I **selenium** 34 (30) mcg

189

tuna

Although tuna is a great source of high-quality protein and vitamins, its essential **omega-3 fatty acids** are the main health boosters. However, this applies to fresh tuna only. Canned tuna has much of its omega-3 content removed in the canning process.

Unlike artery-clogging saturated animal fats, unsaturated fish oils are great for heart health. They improve the ratio between "good" and "bad" cholesterol, make the blood less likely to clot, reduce blood pressure, and help prevent irregular heart rhythms. Tuna is also a good source of folate and vitamin B_6, which together neutralize excessive levels of homocysteine, the heart attack-causing amino acid.

Fish oils have **anti-inflammatory** properties. These, combined with tuna's anti-inflammatory biotin and vitamin B_3 (**niacin**) help rheumatoid arthritis.

Pregnant women should restrict their tuna intake because of fetus-harming mercury levels in the fish.

✳ **storing and serving** Bake, griddle, or broil fresh tuna. When buying canned tuna, choose fish canned in water instead of in oil or its own juices.

griddled tuna and tomato sauce

1 Place **4 x 3½-ounce tuna steaks,** 2 at a time, on a preheated hot griddle, and cook for 3 minutes on each side. Remove and keep warm.

2 Make the tomato sauce by blending together **4 plum tomatoes, 1 teaspoon garlic paste, 1 tablespoon tomato paste,** and **1 tablespoon chopped parsley** for 1 minute. Transfer to a saucepan and cook, uncovered, for 10 minutes.

3 Season with **salt and pepper,** spoon over the cooked tuna and serve. **serves 4**

NUTRITIONAL CONTENT PER 100 G: energy 136 calories | **protein** 24 g | **carbohydrates** 0 g | **fat** 5 g | **fiber** 0 g | **vitamin** B_6 0.38 mg | **potassium** 400 mg | **magnesium** 33 mg | **selenium** 57 mcg

191

NUTRITIONAL CONTENT PER 100 G RAW FILLET: calories 182 calories | protein 18 g | carbohydrates 0 g | fat 12 g | fiber 0 g | potassium 310 mg | calcium 27 mg | selenium 20 mcg

salmon

All fish contain the beneficial **omega-3 fatty acids** that are essential for the body's function, but oily fish contain far more than white fish, and salmon contains more than most.

Research has shown that fish oils are highly beneficial for the heart and help to fight cancer, particularly breast and bowel cancers. (Salmon's anticancer mineral **selenium** may enhance this protective action.)

Moreover, fish oils are "brain food," and including salmon in the diet may improve memory and brain function and help prevent the mental deterioration seen in diseases, such as Alzheimer's. It may also help with depression because fish oils affect levels of serotonin.

The fish oils can reduce inflammation, so people with asthma, rheumatoid arthritis, lupus, and skin conditions, including eczema, may find it helpful to include salmon and other oily fish regularly in their diet.

Canning softens the bones, making them edible, and these provide **calcium, fluoride,** and **phosphorus,** good for helping prevent osteoporosis.

✱ **buying** If possible, choose wild and organic salmon over farmed varieties. Leaner and firmer, these fish contain none of the dyes, antibiotics, or growth-hormone residues found in many farmed fish.

salmon with herb sauce

1 Cook **4 x 2-ounce salmon steaks** under a preheated moderate broiler for 4 minutes on each side.

2 Make the herb sauce by combining **1 tablespoon chopped basil** and **1 tablespoon chopped tarragon** with ¾ **cup plain yogurt.** Season with **salt and pepper.**

3 Serve the salmon with the sauce and **lemon wedges. serves 4**

193

anchovies

Anchovies, which are small oily fish, are an acquired taste and usually used in only small quantities.

They are a rich source of the beneficial fish oils known as **omega-3 fatty acids,** which **lower blood cholesterol** and blood pressure, thereby reducing the risk of heart disease and strokes.

Anchovies may also be helpful for anyone with depression, because the same omega-3 fats affect levels of the mood-altering "feel-good" brain chemical serotonin.

Protein-rich, anchovies contain **calcium, iron,** and **phosphorus** and are a good source of **selenium,** an antioxidant mineral that helps neutralize damaging free radicals, providing some protection against cancer.

Avoid anchovies if you have gout or inflamed joints, because the purines they contain increase the level of uric acid in the joints and exacerbate the pain.

✳ **storing and serving** Most commonly consumed as canned fillets, anchovies are sometimes available fresh or frozen. They are very salty. Rinsing them removes some of the salt (and the oil in which they are canned), but if they are still too salty for your taste, soak them in a little milk for 5 minutes, then rinse and pat them dry with paper towels.

boiled eggs with anchovy toast

1 Boil **4 large eggs** for 4–5 minutes, until softly set.

2 Meanwhile, drain the oil and rinse **8 anchovy fillets** and pat dry with paper towel. Chop finely then beat into **2 tablespoons softened unsalted butter** and season with **pepper.**

3 Spread 4 thick **slices of toast** with the anchovy butter. Cut the toast into fingers and serve with the boiled eggs. **serves 4**

shrimp

Shrimp, sometimes known as prawns, are a low-fat, low-calorie protein, and thus perfect food for dieters. They are high in cholesterol, but it is now known that this has no adverse effect on blood cholesterol levels. On the contrary, the **omega-3 fatty acids** in shrimp can help **lower blood cholesterol** levels as well as reduce blood pressure. They make the blood less likely to clot (a risk factor for strokes and heart attack), making shrimp a really good food for preventing heart disease. Another cardio-protective nutrient in shrimp is **vitamin B$_{12}$**, which regulates the body's levels of the heart attack-causing amino acid, homocysteine.

Eating shrimp is good for brain development and function and for dealing with depression, and they may help reduce aggressive tendencies in some people.

Shrimp can help reduce the risk of cancer, thanks to their levels of the **anticancer** mineral **selenium.**

✽ **storing and serving** Shrimp vary greatly in size and price, but they all taste much the same. Take care not to refreeze shrimp that have been frozen at sea for optimum freshness and thawed for sale. Use shrimp hot or cold.

Kerala shrimp curry

1 Sprinkle ½ **teaspoon ground turmeric** over **1 pound large cooked, peeled shrimp** and set aside.

2 Cut **1 red onion** into fine wedges and deseed and slice **2 green chilies.** Stir-fry in **1 teaspoon vegetable oil** until softened.

3 Add the shrimp, **10 curry leaves** (optional), and ½ **cup coconut milk** and simmer for 5 minutes. Sprinkle over **2 tablespoons lime juice** and season with **salt and pepper.** Scatter with a few **fresh cilantro leaves** and stir once. Serve immediately. **serves 4**

NUTRITIONAL CONTENT PER 100 G BOILED: energy 99 calories I **protein** 23 g I **carbohydrates** 0 g I **fat** 1 g I **fiber** 0 g I **potassium** 260 mg I **calcium** 110 mg I **selenium** 45 mcg

oysters

Oysters have long been considered an aphrodisiac, probably because they are the richest food source of **zinc.** Zinc is essential for sexual health, particularly men's, because it is required for testosterone and sperm production and may help with infertility or impotence. Thanks to both zinc and **selenium,** oysters are great for prostate health and reducing the risk of prostate cancer.

Oysters contain more selenium than other shellfish. This trace mineral helps protect against bowel cancer.

Oysters are good "brain food," and their essential **omega-3 fatty acids** are good for heart health. Although rich in cholesterol, oysters are very low in saturated fat, which is the real culprit when it comes to raised blood cholesterol levels and an increased risk of heart attack.

Oysters may be helpful in fighting fatigue and anemia because of their **blood-boosting iron** content.

✱ **storing and serving** Keep oysters alive until you are ready to cook them by covering them with a damp dish cloth in the refrigerator. Use them within a week, discarding any with open shells because these have died. Serve oysters raw or barely cooked, or you can bake, steam, poach, saute, or broil them.

oriental steamed oysters

1 Remove the top shell from **12 shucked oysters.** Strain the juices through a sieve into a small pan. Wipe out any grit from the shells.

2 Slice **2 scallions** (white parts only), peel and grate **¾-inch fresh piece of ginger root,** slice **1 small garlic clove,** and deseed and slice **1 small red chili.** Add with ¼ **cup sake, 2 tablespoons rice vinegar,** and **2 teaspoons dark soy sauce** to the oyster juices. Warm gently.

3 Arrange the oysters in a large bamboo steamer, cover, and steam for 2 minutes. Put on plates and spoon over the sauce. Serve with **fresh cilantro leaves. serves 4**

NUTRITIONAL CONTENT PER 100 G RAW: energy 65 calories I **protein** 11 g I **carbohydrates** 3 g I **fat** 1 g I **fiber** 0 g I **potassium** 260 mg I **zinc** 59.2 mg I **selenium** 23 mcg I **iron** 5.7 mg

NUTRITIONAL CONTENT PER 1 KG, RAW IN SHELLS: energy 260 calories | protein 52 g | carbohydrates 0 g | fat 6 g | fiber 0 g | potassium 280 mg | zinc 6 mg | selenium 90 mcg

mussels

Like most seafood, mussels are rich in the cardio-protective **omega-3 fatty acids,** which are vital for the body. In addition to protecting the heart and enhancing brain function, omega-3 fats are **anti-inflammatory** agents and may help people with asthma, rheumatoid arthritis, psoriasis, and inflammatory bowel disease (IBS).

Including mussels in the diet is especially beneficial for menstruating women and new mothers and for middle-aged and elderly men. This is because mussels are rich in both **iron,** which is good for combating fatigue and anemia, and **zinc,** which is required for male sexual function and prostate health.

Like a lot of seafood, mussels also contain **iodine,** which is needed for healthy thyroid function, and **vitamin E** and **selenium,** which protect cells and tissues from damage by free radicals and are, therefore, important for fighting cancer.

✱ **storing and serving** Keep live mussels in the refrigerator covered with a damp dish cloth. Use them within a week, discarding any with open shells. Do not overcook mussels because this toughens them. Serve them, in or out of their shells, in seafood soups, stews, and salads, or simply bake them in their shells.

mussel gratin

1 Heat **4 tablespoons white wine** in a saucepan until bubbling. Clean, debeard and add **1 pound mussels.** Cover and cook for 4–5 minutes. Drain, reserving cooking juices. Discard any closed shells.

2 Remove the mussels from their shells. Break the shells apart and arrange half of them on a foil-lined broiler rack. Place a mussel in each.

3 Blend ⅓ **cup crème fraîche or sour cream** with 4 tablespoons of cooking juices. Spoon into the shells.

4 Melt **4 tablespoons butter** in a frying pan. Stir in **2 crushed garlic cloves, 1½ cups fresh bread crumbs, 4 tablespoons chopped mixed herbs,** and season. Spoon over the mussels and broil until lightly toasted.

serves 4

201

scallops

Scallops have heart-protective properties due to their high levels of **omega-3 fatty acids** and vitamin B_{12} and of magnesium and **potassium,** which help regulate blood-pressure levels. Vitamin B_{12} reduces a harmful buildup of the amino acid homocysteine, high levels of which increase the risk of stroke and heart attack.

The omega-3 fatty acids in seafood are unsaturated fats that improve the ratio of "good" and "bad" cholesterol. They reduce high blood pressure, make the blood less likely to clot, and help regulate the heart beat.

Eating scallops may **improve memory** and protect against age-related dementia. In addition, the protein in scallops and oysters contains the amino acid tyrosine, which produces mentally energizing chemicals that enhance attentiveness and the speed of reactions.

Scallops are also good for protecting against cancer because of their high levels of **anticancer selenium.**

✻ storing and serving Scallops are usually sold removed from their shells. They are highly perishable and should be refrigerated and eaten on the day of purchase. Scallops need only a few minutes' cooking, or they will become tough.

seared scallops with lime-dressed salad

1 Clean **16 large scallops** and dry them well with paper towel to remove excess water. Cook on a preheated hot griddle for 3 minutes on each side.

2 Mix together the grated rind and juice of **2 limes, 3 tablespoons olive oil,** and a **bunch of chopped dill.** Season with **salt and pepper.**

3 Toss a large bag of **mixed lettuce leaves** in the lime dressing and arrange on 4 plates. Plate the scallops on top and garnish with a little of the dressing. **serves 4**

NUTRITIONAL CONTENT PER 100 G STEAMED NO SHELL: energy 118 calories | **protein** 23 g | **carbohydrates** 3 g | **fat** 1 g | **fiber** 0 g | **potassium** 240 mg | **magnesium** 38 mg | **zinc** 2.4 mg

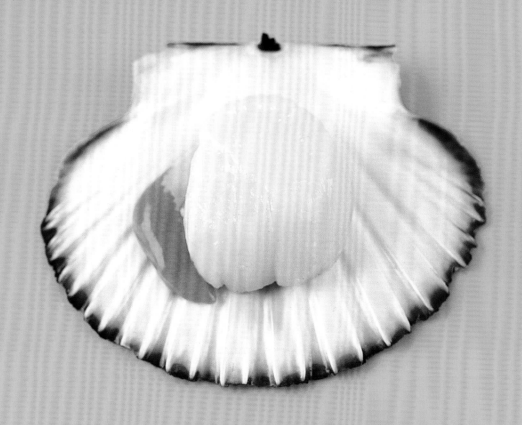

203

brown rice

Unlike white rice, which is stripped of its layers and, therefore, nutrients during processing, brown rice is a natural whole grain with a high-fiber content.

Fiber helps the digestive system function efficiently, protecting against bowel cancer by quickly conveying waste matter out of the body. Brown rice also contains the antioxidant **anticancer** trace mineral **selenium,** which is protective against bowel and prostate cancers.

Eating brown rice is good for the heart because both the fiber and a compound in its bran (the outer layer) called **orysanol** help reduce the body's levels of "bad" cholesterol. This cholesterol can clog arteries, resulting in strokes and heart attacks.

The fiber makes brown rice a great source of slow-burning energy and helps stabilize blood sugar levels, so is particularly good for diabetics and athletes.

✱ **storing and serving** Because its natural oils can turn rancid, brown rice is best kept in an airtight container in the refrigerator. Soaking brown rice before use reduces the cooking time. To retain the nutrients, use the same water for cooking, and don't cook with excess water that then has to be drained.

brown rice pudding with raisins and almonds

1 Rinse ⅓ **cup brown rice** and cook for 15 minutes. Drain, then bring slowly to a boil with **4 cups milk** and **2 tablespoons soft light brown sugar.**

2 Pour into a buttered, ovenproof 2-quart dish. Add ⅓ **cup raisins** and stir. Sprinkle over ½ **teaspoon grated nutmeg** and dot with **1 tablespoon butter.**

3 Cook in a preheated oven set to 350°F, for 1½–2 hours, stirring twice. Sprinkle with chopped **stem ginger** and **flaked almonds.** Serve with crème fraîche or plain yogurt. **serves 4–6**

NUTRITIONAL CONTENT PER 100 G BOILED: energy 140 calories I **protein** 3 g I **carbohydrates** 32 g I **fat** 1 g I **fiber** 1.5 g I **potassium** 99 mg I **magnesium** 43 mg I **calcium** 4 mg

buckwheat

Often categorized as a grain, buckwheat is actually a seed. Free of gluten, it is suitable for people who have celiac disease.

The flavonoids in buckwheat help protect against heart disease. These antioxidant compounds, rutin in particular, help prevent blood clots and **reduce levels of blood cholesterol,** as well as lower high blood pressure. Rutin strengthens and tones blood vessels, so buckwheat can help people with varicose veins.

Buckwheat may help prevent cancer, because it contains rutin and quercetin, together with the free radical-fighting **vitamin E.** Its high-fiber content stimulates the digestive tract into removing potentially toxic substances before they can cause harmful tumors.

Buckwheat can help prevent and manage diabetes, because it is a good source of slow-release energy, which stops fluctuating blood sugar levels.

✱ **storing and serving** Store buckwheat in an airtight container in a cupboard or in the refrigerator. Use ground buckwheat to make a porridgelike breakfast cereal, and serve the whole kernels like rice.

Breton crepes

1 Lightly beat **2 eggs, 1 tablespoon vegetable oil,** and **½ cup beer.**

2 Sift **1 cup buckwheat flour** into a bowl, then gradually add the liquid, whisking to form a smooth batter. Thin with ¾ **cup water** and whisk again. Leave to stand for 10 minutes.

3 Brush a 5½-inch frying pan with **vegetable oil** and heat. Coat the base of the pan with batter and tip from side to side to cover the base before the mixture sets. Cook on each side for 30 seconds, flipping inbetween. Remove the crepes from the pan, cover, and keep warm while you cook the remainder. Serve with ratatouille, if you want. **makes about 15**

NUTRITIONAL CONTENT PER 100 G RAW: energy 364 calories **I protein** 8 g **I carbohydrates** 85 g **I fat** 2 g **I fiber** 2 g **I potassium** 220 mg **I magnesium** 48 mg **I calcium** 12 mg **I iron** 2 mg

NUTRITIONAL CONTENT PER 100 G RAW: energy 309 calories I protein 14 g I carbohydrates 56 g I fat 5 g I fiber 6 g I vitamin E 4.87 mg I magnesium 210 mg I manganese 2.25 mg

quinoa

The ancient Incas regarded quinoa as a sacred food, and each season the emperor was responsible for planting the first seed.

Quinoa is a seed—not a grain—but it has many of the qualities of grain, being a low-fat, energizing, cancer-preventing, heart-protecting whole food. An excellent source of **complete protein,** on a par with milk, quinoa is great for vegetarians and vegans.

Eating quinoa regularly may assist people with migraine because the **magnesium** it contains relaxes blood vessels and improves blood flow. The vitamin B_2 (riboflavin) may help reduce the frequency of attacks.

Whole "grains," such as quinoa, have a role in cancer prevention, thanks to their high-fiber levels, (which help protect against bowel cancer), lignans (plant hormones thought to protect against hormone-related cancers), and free radical-fighting manganese and copper.

Eating quinoa regularly can help keep the heart healthy, because the grain's fiber lowers cholesterol.

✿ **storing and serving** Store quinoa in an airtight container in a cupboard or in the refrigerator. Rinse well to remove any residue of its inedible coating. Dry-fry quinoa before cooking to enhance its nutty flavor, then cook as you would rice.

quinoa coconut ice cream

1 Put ½ **cup quinoa** and ¾ **cup rice milk** in a saucepan, bring to a boil, and simmer gently for 15 minutes. Beat in ¾ **cup soya milk.** Simmer for another 5 minutes. Add ¼ **cup maple syrup** and **1 cup coconut milk** and beat again.

2 Still beating, add ½ **cup rapeseed oil, 1 teaspoon vanilla extract, 1 tablespoon lemon juice,** and **1 chopped banana,** and beat until smooth. Transfer to an airtight container and freeze for 12 hours, stirring every hour or two to break up any ice crystals. **serves 4**

wheat germ

Wheat germ is the most nutritious part of the wheat grain, yet is discarded in the refining process that makes white flour. A highly concentrated source of nutrients, it contains protein, B vitamins such as **folate, vitamin E, zinc, selenium, iron,** and magnesium.

Because wheat germ is such a good source of fiber, it can ease constipation and by ensuring the smooth and efficient operation of the digestive tract, it helps prevent bowel cancer. Selenium has effective **anticancer** properties, too.

Wheat germ is a good source of vitamin E, which is linked to a reduced risk of stroke, heart disease, and cancer. It is also particularly important for maintaining healthy skin, and a healthy heart, and circulation, nerves, muscles, and red blood cells.

The folate in wheat germ helps to protect unborn children from spina bifida. Wheat germ can also prevent fatigue and anemia because the folate works with iron, magnesium, and zinc to build red blood cells.

✱ **storing and serving** Because of its fat content, wheat germ needs to be stored in the refrigerator. Use in baking, on yogurt, breakfast cereal, or in drinks.

wheat germ, pineapple, and banana booster

1 Toast **2 tablespoons wheat germ** and **1 tablespoon sesame seeds** under a broiler, stirring a couple of times until the sesame seeds have begun to turn golden. Remove from the broiler and let cool.

2 Roughly slice **2 bananas** and blend to a rough puree with **½ cup pineapple chunks.**

3 Add **2 cups apple juice** and blend to a fairly smooth juice. Add **1¼ cups plain yogurt** and the cooked wheat germ and sesame seeds, blend again, and serve. **serves 4**

NUTRITIONAL CONTENT PER 100 G RAW: energy 357 calories | **protein** 27 g | **carbohydrates** 45 g | **fat** 9 g | **fiber** 16 g | **vitamin E** 22 mg | **magnesium** 270 mg | **iron** 8.5 mg | **zinc** 17 mg

chickpeas

Also known as garbanzo beans and ceci, chickpeas were cultivated as long ago as 4000 B.C. They are a good source of protein and fiber, as well as **energy-producing iron** and manganese.

Like all legumes, chickpeas are ideal for diabetics because the fiber prevents blood sugar levels from rising too quickly after a meal. The fiber is great for the digestive system, too, helping prevent constipation, diverticulosis, and irritable bowel syndrome (IBS). It may also reduce the risk of bowel cancer.

The soluble fiber in chickpeas, together with **folate, and** magnesium offers protection against heart disease.

In addition, chickpeas are a good source of molybdenum, a detoxifying trace mineral that helps rid the body of sulfites. These are commonly used food preservatives, to which some people are particularly sensitive.

✱ storing and serving Store dried chickpeas in an airtight container for up to a year. Once cooked, they can be kept in the refrigerator for a few days or frozen. Add to salads and dips, Indian dishes, and soups.

spiced chickpea salad

1 Finely chop **1 red onion,** then heat **1 tablespoon olive oil** in a heavy-based saucepan and cook the onion for 5 minutes, or until softened.

2 Add **1 teaspoon ground turmeric** and **2 teaspoons cumin seeds** and cook, stirring, for 1–2 minutes. Skin and roughly chop **2 medium tomatoes.** Drain a **13-ounce can chickpeas,** rinse them, and add to the pan with the tomatoes and **2 teaspoons lemon juice** and **salt and pepper.** Cook for a further 2–3 minutes.

3 Stir in **2 tablespoons chopped fresh cilantro. serves 2**

NUTRITIONAL CONTENT PER 100 G CANNED, DRAINED WEIGHT: energy
115 calories | **protein** 7 g | **carbohydrates** 16 g | **fat** 3 g | **fiber** 4 g | **vitamin E** 1.55 mg | **calcium** 43 mcg

213

lentils

The seeds of a leguminous plant, lentils come in various colors and sizes. Among vegetables, they are second only to soy beans for protein content and so an excellent option for vegetarians, but they need to be eaten with a complementary protein, such as grains.

Because they are high in fiber, lentils keep you feeling full for longer, which makes them useful for dieters, especially because they are low in fat, and they provide slow-burning energy to keep you going (which also makes them ideal for diabetics). The cholesterol-lowering fiber also means that lentils are excellent for the heart as well as the digestive system.

Lentils contain a good range of nutrients (green and brown lentils even more so than red ones). These include **iron,** useful for those prone to anemia, some good minerals for bone health, and a number of B vitamins, which help to stabilize blood pressure.

Lentils have **anti-inflammatory** properties so are a good food for people with rheumatoid arthritis.

✱ storing and serving Some brands of lentils are ready to use, but most lentils need thorough rinsing and picking over to remove dust and grit before soaking and cooking. Canned lentils are convenient but not quite as nutritious as dried ones.

dhal

1 Briefly fry **6 cloves, 6 cardamoms,** and **1 inch cinnamon stick** in **4 tablespoons olive oil.**

2 Chop **1 onion** and fry until translucent. Next, finely chop **1 green chili,** and chop a **1-inch piece of fresh ginger root** and **1 garlic clove.** Add them all to the pan with **½ teaspoon garam masala.** Cook for 5 minutes.

3 Stir in **1 cup lentils** and fry for 1 minute. Add **salt** and sufficient water to come about 1¼ inches above the lentils. Bring to a boil, cover, and simmer for 20 minutes. Sprinkle over **4 tablespoons lemon juice,** stir and serve. **serves 4**

215

beans

Beans, lentils, and chickpeas are all legumes with similar health-boosting properties. A **low-fat, filling protein food** with slow-release sugars, beans are particularly good for the digestive system. One study even suggests that a serving of beans four times a week may **reduce the risk of heart disease** by 22 percent.

Beans, usually available dried, are edible seeds. They are highly nutritious, resulting in the expression to be **"full of beans,"** meaning to be lively. Dried beans, such as aduki, mung, and soy beans, can be sprouted, which makes them rich in both B and C vitamins.

Beans also contain phytoestrogens, which can help tackle erratic periods and premenstrual syndrome (PMS) and relieve some menopausal symptoms.

Beans contain lignans and isoflavones, which help prevent hormone-dependent cancers.

✱ **storing and serving** Store dried beans in airtight containers in the cupboard. Cook them to serve as a simple side dish or use them in thick soups, stews, and casseroles. Mash them for use in dips and pâtés or add them to salads.

cannellini bean and sun-dried tomato salad

1 Heat **2 tablespoons olive oil** in a frying pan. Add **1 crushed garlic clove** and saute until golden. Remove from pan.

2 Drain and rinse **14-ounce can cannellini beans,** place in a mixing bowl, and stir in the garlic. Add **1 sliced red onion, ¾ cup chopped sun-dried tomatoes (drained from their oil), 1 tablespoon chopped black olives, 2 teaspoons chopped capers, 2 teaspoons chopped thyme, 1 tablespoon parsley leaves, 1 tablespoon extra virgin olive oil, 1 tablespoon lemon juice, salt and pepper,** and mix well. **serves 4**

NUTRITIONAL CONTENT PER 100 G CANNELLINI BEANS, CANNED : energy 94 calories | **protein** 7 g | **carbohydrates** 14 g | **fat** 0 g | **fiber** 6 g | **calcium** 65 mg | **iron** 2.5 mg

217

chilies

Chili peppers, which come in a range of sizes, shapes, colors and heat levels, contain the antioxidant vitamins A (beta-carotene), C, and E, plus **folate** and **potassium.** They are, therefore, good for general health and for protecting the heart.

Countless healing properties have been attributed to chilies, but many claims have yet to be validated. What is known is that capsaicin, which accounts for the "heat" of chilies, can help prevent dangerous blood clots and help with weight loss, because capsaicin both suppresses the appetite and helps to boost metabolism.

The World Health Organization (WHO) has reported a link between capsaicin-rich diets and reduced death rates from cancer.

Research from Australia shows chilies have an effect on insulin so are good for regulating blood sugar levels.

✱ **storing and serving** Keep fresh chilies in the refrigerator, and dried chilies and chili powder in airtight jars, away from the heat and light of cooking. Removing the seeds and membranes of fresh chilies will minimize their heat but will also remove the health-boosting capsaicin.

fresh chili chutney

1 Puree **6 fresh green chilies** with **1 cup vinegar** and transfer to a hot, dry sterilized jar.

2 Top up with vinegar to prevent a mold from forming and tightly cover the jar. The chutney will change in color from bright to dark green in about 1–2 weeks but will keep indefinitely. **makes about 1 cup**

NUTRITIONAL CONTENT PER 100 G RAW: energy 20 calories I **protein** 3 g I **carbohydrates** 1 g I **fat** 1 g I **fiber** 2 g I **vitamin C** 120 mg I **carotene** 175 mcg I **folate** 29 mcg I **potassium** 220 mg

ginger

Ginger is a centuries-old digestive aid and a popular remedy for nausea, particularly travel sickness and morning sickness. It can also help relieve indigestion and heartburn and is useful for treating coughs, colds, and flulike symptoms.

The health-boosting properties of ginger appear to be due to its powerful gingerols. These act as **anti-inflammatory** agents, so ginger can reduce the pain and swelling of rheumatism and arthritis and may help alleviate asthma, painful periods, and migraines.

The gingerol compounds appear to be antioxidants, and initial studies suggest that they may provide some protection against cancer. Similarly, ginger is believed by some to lower cholesterol and protect against heart disease, but more research is required.

Ginger boosts the metabolism, so dieters may find it useful for accelerating calorie burning.

✱ storing and serving Fresh unpeeled ginger root will keep for up to two weeks in the refrigerator and up to six months if frozen. Use fresh ginger in Indian dishes, stir-fries, and salad dressings.

scallions and ginger rice

1 Wash **1½ cups long-grain rice.** Transfer to a pan with **1 teaspoon salt, 3 bruised cardamom pods,** and **2½ cups water.** Simmer over a low heat for 5 minutes. Cover tightly and cook for 5 minutes until tender.

2 Deseed and chop **1 green chili,** crush **2 garlic cloves,** thinly slice **2 zucchini,** and chop a **bunch of scallions.** Stir-fry in **2 tablespoons olive oil** with **1 tablespoon grated fresh ginger** for 1 minute. Add the rice, **2 tablespoons chopped fresh cilantro, 2 tablespoons light soy sauce,** and **1 tablespoon lemon juice.** Stir over a low heat for 2 minutes. **serves 4**

NUTRITIONAL CONTENT PER 100 G ROOT, RAW: energy 38 calories | **protein** 1 g | **carbohydrates** 7 g | **fat** 1 g | **fiber** 2 g | **vitamin C** 4 mg | **potassium** 320 mg | **magnesium** 35 mg

garlic

Cultivated as early as 2000 B.C. in Mesopotamia and Egypt, garlic was believed by the ancient Greeks and Romans to possess magical properties.

Garlic contains powerful sulfurous compounds thought to slow or prevent the growth of cancer and to **stimulate the liver's detoxification function.** The same compounds, plus vitamins B_6 and C and manganese and **selenium,** make garlic highly protective toward the heart. Eating garlic regularly can help keep arteries clear and lower high cholesterol levels; it also reduces the risk of blood clotting and reduces high blood pressure.

Garlic is a natural antibiotic and, taken regularly, can build up resistance to infection. It is a decongestant, helping to relieve the symptoms of colds, coughs, and flu. It is also an **anti-inflammatory** and may help protect against asthma and rheumatoid arthritis.

✱ storing and serving Store fresh garlic in an uncovered container away from heat and sunlight. An unbroken bulb will keep for a couple of months. Eating a clove a day is recommended by health experts—try chewing parsley or coffee beans to counteract the smell.

garlic and almond soup

1 Tear **4 slices bread** into small pieces, put in a bowl and cover with water. In another bowl, cover **⅔ cup raisins** with water. Let stand to soak for 30–60 minutes.

2 Remove the bread from the water and squeeze dry. Blend to a smooth paste with **1 cup toasted blanched almonds.**

3 Add **3 tablespoons olive oil, 3 crushed garlic cloves,** the raisins, and **4 cups milk** (or water). Blend to make a smooth soup. Chill for 2–3 hours before serving in small bowls. **serves 6**

NUTRITIONAL CONTENT PER 100 G RAW: energy 98 calories I **protein** 8 g I **carbohydrates** 16 g I **fat** 1 g I **fiber** 4 g I **vitamin** B_6 0.38 mg I **manganese** 0.5 mg I **selenium** 2 mcg

223

fresh herbs

A recent study by the US Department of Agriculture found thyme, rosemary, sage, peppermint, and particularly oregano, also known as wild marjoram, to be **highly antioxidant.** In fact, oregano has four times more free radical-fighting antioxidants than blueberries.

Rosemary can help **boost the immune system.** It is especially useful at exam time because it increases blood flow to the brain, improving concentration. The menthol in peppermint stops muscle spasm, so it helps treat indigestion, heartburn, flatulence, and nausea.

Basil and sage are **anti-inflammatories.** Both can help relieve the symptoms of rheumatoid arthritis, asthma, and inflammatory bowel conditions. Basil and thyme have antibacterial qualities, and adding either to salad dressings can help remove a diarrhea-causing bacteria from lettuce leaves. Parsley helps kidney function, relieves gout, and combats anemia.

✱ storing and serving Fresh herbs are more health-boosting than dried ones, so substitute 1 tablespoon chopped fresh herb for 1 teaspoon of the dried equivalent whenever possible in cooking. Fresh herbs freeze well if you have a surplus.

herby risotto

1 Finely chop **1 onion** and **1 garlic clove.** Saute in **4 tablespoons butter** with **2 tablespoons olive oil** for 5 minutes.

2 Add **1½ cups risotto rice** and stir well to coat the grains. Add **4¼ cups hot vegetable stock,** a ladleful at a time, stirring until each addition is absorbed. Add the stock and cook until the rice is creamy but the grains are firm.

3 Mix in handful each of chopped **parsley, basil, oregano, and thyme, 6 tablespoons butter,** and **½ cup grated Toma cheese or other semi-hard cheese.** Season with **salt and pepper** and stir well. Cover and let stand for a few minutes before serving. **serves 4**

NUTRITIONAL CONTENT PER 100 G FRESH BASIL (OREGANO): energy 40 (66) calories | **protein** 3 (2) g | **carbohydrates** 5 (10) g | **fat** 1 (2) g | **fiber** 0 (0) g | **potassium** 300 (330) mg

225

horseradish

Thanks to its strong volatile oils, which are similar to those found in mustard, horseradish has an intensity of flavor strong enough to bring tears to the eyes.

Its pungency explains why horseradish can relieve cold symptoms and congested sinuses by dissolving mucus. It can also relieve water retention, or bloating, and may provide some relief from rheumatism.

Its **antibiotic properties** mean horseradish can fight infections, such as tonsillitis, and protect the gut from bacteria, including listeria and *E. coli*.

Horseradish is a member of the brassica family and contains the phytochemicals called **glucosinolates,** which have been shown to fight cancer by suppressing tumor growths. Glucosinolates also increase the liver's ability to detoxify.

✱ **storing and serving** Horseradish is most commonly available as horseradish sauce or as prepared horseradish, which is made from shredded and pounded horseradish mixed with vinegar. Creamed horseradish is a creamier version. Once opened, store prepared and creamed horseradish in the refrigerator for up to six months. Traditionally paired with roast beef, horseradish also goes well with smoked salmon and adds a zing to mashed potato, cream cheese, or mayonnaise.

horseradish mash

1 Peel and dice **4 medium (1½ pounds) potatoes** and cook in boiling water for about 20 minutes, or until tender. Drain well and return to the pan.

2 Add **4 tablespoons butter,** **⅔ cup light cream,** and **2–3 tablespoons freshly grated horseradish** and mash well. Season with **salt and pepper** and serve. **serves 4**

227

chicken and turkey

As long as you avoid eating the skin, chicken and turkey are healthy alternatives to red meat.

If you have trouble sleeping, try eating poultry in the evening. Both chicken and turkey are rich in an amino acid called tryptophan, which helps regulate sleep. Tryptophan can also lift the spirits and the **zinc** in turkey can assist in combating depression and anxiety.

Eating poultry may help prevent cancer, because chicken and, to a lesser extent, turkey are good sources of two **anticancer** nutrients, **niacin** and **selenium.**

Chicken, which is a good source of the B vitamins required by the brain for memory maintenance, is also good for preventing forgetfulness and age-related mental decline. Indeed, its vitamin B_3 (niacin) content may help protect against Alzheimer's disease.

✱ **storing and serving** Keep raw poultry closely wrapped in the refrigerator to avoid contaminating other foods, and wash your hands and utensils well after handling it. To avoid the risk of infection, chicken and turkey should always be cooked completely through until no pink meat is left and any juices run clear.

chicken with rosemary and garlic

1 Mix together **2 tablespoons olive oil, 2 tablespoons white wine vinegar, 2 tablespoons chopped rosemary, 3 crushed garlic cloves, 1 teaspoon paprika,** and the pared rind of **1 lemon,** and season with **salt and pepper. Add 4 skinless chicken breasts** (cut into long thin strips) and mix well. Let marinate for 10 minutes.

2 Cook the chicken and the marinade over a moderate heat, stirring constantly, for 15 minutes.

3 Stir in a **handful of chopped flat leaf parsley** immediately before serving. **serves 4**

NUTRITIONAL CONTENT PER 100 G RAW BREAST CHICKEN (TURKEY): energy 116 (103) calories | **protein** 22 (23) g | **carbohydrates** 0 (0) g | **fat** 3 (1) g | **fiber** 0 (0) g | **zinc** 0.7 (1.2) mg

229

game fowl

Traditionally hunted in the wild, game birds are now often commercially reared. Because they forage for their food, they are more active and, therefore, leaner than domestic birds. Their fat is mainly monounsaturated.

Guinea fowl meat is a good source of heart-protective vitamin B_6 and of two **anticancer** nutrients, **selenium** and **niacin.**

Pheasant and partridge are excellent sources of **iron,** partridge providing about three times as much as beef. Lack of iron can cause anemia and reduced concentration. Pheasant and partridge also provide **phosphorus** and **calcium,** essential for the formation of strong bones; **potassium,** which helps prevent high blood pressure; and vitamin B_6 and **folate,** both of which help reduce excess levels of homocysteine, a risk factor for heart attacks.

Partridge contains high levels of sulfur, the "beauty mineral," essential for glossy hair, skin, and nails.

✱ **storing and serving** Game birds can easily dry out, so require basting while roasting. Older birds are tougher and are best casseroled slowly.

grilled guinea fowl

1 Put **4 boneless guinea fowl breasts** on a lightly oiled broiler pan, brush with **olive oil,** and season with **salt and pepper.** Place the pan under a preheated hot broiler and cook for 10 minutes on each side.

2 Blend **3 crushed garlic cloves, 4 chopped anchovy fillets,** a large **handful of flat leaf parsley,** a handful each of **rocket, sorrel,** and **basil** leaves, and **2 tablespoons lemon juice.** With the motor running, slowly drizzle in ½ **cup olive oil.** Season and blend again.

3 Serve the guinea fowl with the herb sauce. **serves 4**

NUTRITIONAL CONTENT PER 100 G RAW GUINEA FOWL (ROAST PHEASANT):
energy 110 (213) calories | **protein** 21 (32) g | **carbohydrates** 0 (0) g | **fat** 3 (9) g | **fiber** 0 (0) g

lean red meat

In contrast to greasy hamburgers, big steaks dripping with fat, and roast pork with crispy crackling, lean beef, lamb, or pork eaten in moderation can boost your health. Lean red meat is a good source of protein, **zinc, selenium,** and **iron,** plus vitamins B_3 (**niacin**), B_6 and B_{12}, which can all help keep the heart in good shape.

B vitamins are heart protective because they reduce excess levels of an amino acid called homocysteine, which can cause strokes and heart attacks. Vitamin B_3 (niacin), B_{12} and selenium are all linked with a reduced risk of cancer, particularly bowel cancer.

Eating lean meat can **boost the immune system,** thanks to the high levels of **zinc,** which is important for sexual health, prostate health, and wound healing.

✱ **choosing lean meat** Opt for the leanest cuts of meat (those from the animal's legs) and always remove all visible fat. Pork is often regarded as a fatty meat, but pork escalopes actually have less saturated fat than beef or lamb and are almost on a par with chicken for their fat content. Buy organic meat to avoid the residues of growth hormones and antibiotics found in nonorganic meat.

green peppercorn steak

1 Cook **4 x 3-ounce fillet steaks** for 2–3 minutes on each side on a preheated hot griddle pan. Remove from the pan and keep hot.

2 Add **1 tablespoon green peppercorns** in brine, drained, **2 tablespoons light soy sauce, 1 teaspoon balsamic vinegar,** and **8 halved cherry tomatoes** to the griddle pan. Allow the liquids to sizzle for 2 minutes, or until the tomatoes are soft.

3 Spoon the sauce over the steaks and garnish with **thyme sprigs. serves 4**

NUTRITIONAL CONTENT PER 100 G LEAN RAW BEEF: energy 123 calories I **protein** 17 g I **carbohydrates** 0 g I **fat** 5 g I **fiber** 0 g I **folate** 10 mcg I **iron** 2.1 mg I **zinc** 4.3 mg I **selenium** 3 mcg

233

234

NUTRITIONAL CONTENT PER 100 G RAW: energy 103 calories I protein 22 g I carbohydrates 0 g I fat 2 g I fiber 0 g I potassium 340 mg I iron 3.3 mg I selenium 9 mcg I zinc 2.4 mg

venison

Iron-rich venison is the healthiest of the red meats, containing less than half the saturated fat of lean beef. In fact, venison's **low-calorie, low-fat,** and **high-protein** profile is similar to that of chicken and salmon. Venison is also a surprising source of essential **omega-3 fatty acids.** These "good" fats reduce the risk factors (high cholesterol levels and blood clots) for stroke and heart attacks. They also support brain health and development and can help deal with depression.

A source of **iron,** venison is good for those prone to fatigue and anemia and in need of an iron boost.

Venison also provides a number of B vitamins, which are important for producing energy. Two of these, vitamins B_6 and B_{12}, have cardio-protective properties, and vitamin B_{12} may help protect against osteoporosis and bowel cancer.

✱ **storing and serving** Venison is available as whole joints, steaks, chops, or ground meat. Store it according to whether it is fresh or frozen. You can substitute venison for beef in virtually any recipe. Use it in hearty casseroles, pasta dishes, or in kebabs for the barbecue. Overcooking it will toughen it.

griddled venison steaks with red fruit sauce

1 Mix together **1 teaspoon crushed juniper berries** and a **pinch of pepper** and spread over both sides of **4 x 6-ounce venison steaks** (fillet or loin). Leave overnight.

2 Put ½ **cup red currant jelly,** **1 cup cranberries,** the grated rind and juice of **1 orange,** and **2 tablespoons red wine** in a small saucepan. Simmer gently for 10 minutes, stirring constantly.

3 Griddle the venison steaks for 3 minutes on each side for rare or 5 minutes for well done. Serve with the sauce and garnish with **shredded orange rind. serves 4**

NUTRITIONAL CONTENT PER 100 G RAW LAMB (CALF): calories 179 (153) calories | **protein** 20 (20) g | **carbohydrates** 2 (2) g | **fat** 10 (7) g | **fiber** 0 (0) g | **folate** 220 (240) g | **iron** 9 (8) mg

liver

Liver is well known for being a rich source of **iron,** which helps prevent or cure anemia. It also contains vitamins B_1, B_2, B_6 and B_{12}, which are necessary for the formation of hemoglobin and for brain function.

Because the vitamin A levels in farmed liver are very high, pregnant women should not eat liver or liver products, because it could harm the developing fetus. However, both foods are recommended after the birth, especially for breastfeeding mothers.

Eating liver may provide some protection against heart disease and cancer because it is an excellent source of the cardio-protective vitamin B_{12} and **folate,** as well as the antioxidant minerals **zinc, selenium,** and copper, which protect against damaging free radicals and may prevent prostate cancer.

Although liver contains more fat than lean meat, most of this is in the form of polyunsaturated fats, so it is not harmful and is unlikely to raise blood cholesterol levels.

✱ **buying organic** Because the liver is the organ responsible for filtering toxins, toxic substances are likely to collect here. It, therefore, makes sense to eat only liver from an organically reared animal to avoid consuming pesticides or other chemical residues.

quick liver one-pot

1 Thinly slice **2 onions** and **3 carrots** and cook in **1 tablespoon olive oil** with **4 slices of lean bacon** over a low heat for 10 minutes.

2 Add **1 tablespoon red currant jelly** and **1 tablespoon tomato paste** and cook for a further 2 minutes, stirring occasionally.

3 Add **1 pound lamb's liver,** cover, and let cook for about 5 minutes. Stir, season with **salt and pepper,** return the cover, and cook for a further 2–3 minutes. Serve immediately with mashed potatoes and a selection of green vegetables. **serves 4**

tea

The subject of a great deal of research, tea offers powerful antioxidant properties. Black, oolong, and green teas all come from the same plant, but their leaves are processed differently.

The least processed of the three, green tea, is the most beneficial. Its main health-boosting ingredients are tannins and catechins, antioxidants with effective cancer-prevention and heart-protective properties.

Numerous studies have shown that green tea-drinking populations have a reduced risk of a huge range of disorders and diseases. Besides combating cancer and heart disease, drinking green tea can lower blood sugar levels and help prevent type 2 (late-onset) diabetes. It may have some effect on the AIDS virus, and it can help prevent osteoporosis.

Green tea is useful for treating diarrhea and for killing the bacteria responsible for stomach upset.

Both green and black teas help combat the flu virus.

✱ **storing and serving** Keep tea in a cupboard. Use boiling water for black and oolong tea, but use slightly cooler water for green tea.

Earl Grey brûlée

1 Bring **2½ cups light cream** to a boil. Stir in **8 teaspoons Earl Grey tea leaves.** Stand for 15 minutes.

2 Beat together **8 egg yolks** and **½ cup sugar.** Reheat the tea-flavored cream and stir it into the egg mixture a little at a time.

3 Strain the custard into 6 ramekins in a roasting pan. Pour warm water into the pan to come halfway up the sides of the dishes and bake in a preheated oven set to 350°F, for 20–25 minutes.

4 Let cool, then chill for 3–4 hours. Before serving, sprinkle the tops with ¼ cup sugar. Caramelize with a blowtorch, and serve at room temperature. **serves 6**

NUTRITIONAL CONTENT PER ½ CUP INFUSED, BLACK OR GREEN: energy 0 calories | **protein** 0.1 g | **carbohydrates** 0 g | **fat** 0 g | **fiber** 0 g | **potassium** 17 mg (analysis done using distilled water – mineral content will vary according to local water used)

239

glossary

glossary

Absorption Process by which nutrients are taken from the intestine into the bloodstream and into cells.

ACE vitamins Vitamins A, C, and E, which are especially renowned for their strong antioxidant powers.

Additives The term commonly used to refer to synthetic colorings or preservatives, often added to processed food to enhance the appearance and shelf life of the final product.

Allicin A beneficial sulfurous compound found in garlic that dilates blood vessels, thereby reducing the risk of blood clots and helping protect the heart.

Alpha-carotene A type of carotenoid found in carrots and other vegetables. A powerful antioxidant, it helps protect cells from the damage inflicted by free radicals and, like beta-carotene, can be converted in the body to vitamin A.

Alpha-linolenic acid An omega-3 essential fatty acid, vital for the body's health.

Alzheimer's disease A disease that kills brain cells, causing progressive memory loss and dementia. Drug treatment appears to slow progression of the disease but there is currently no cure.

Amino acids The 20 different building blocks of proteins. Some of them—for example asparagine and glutamine—can be synthesized in our bodies. The others (known as the essential amino acids) have to be obtained from protein foods in the diet, such as meat, fish, beans, and lentils. Essential amino acids include leucine, tryptophan, lysine, and tyrosine.

Anaemia A condition in which the blood's oxygen-carrying capacity is lessened. Anaemia is caused by various conditions, including excessive menstrual bleeding and lack of iron, vitamin B_{12} or folate in the diet. The symptoms include pallor, weakness and fatigue, depression, and low resistance to infections.

Anthocyanidins A group of flavonoids found in red, purple, and blue fruits and vegetables.

Antibacterial The ability to kill bacteria, but not viruses.

Antibodies Proteins produced by the immune system in response to "foreign" invaders (antigens), such as those belonging to viruses.

Following exposure to a particular infection, the body "remembers" the foreign protein and can fight off the infection more quickly next time.

Anti-inflammatory
The ability to reduce inflammation.

Antimicrobial The ability to kill both bacteria and viruses.

Antioxidants Beneficial natural substances found in foods that rid the body of the damaging free radicals that cause oxidation, resulting in better general health and delayed aging.

Antiseptic The ability to prevent the growth or spread of microorganisms, inhibiting their action but not killing them.

Antiviral The ability to kill viruses, but not bacteria.

Ascorbic acid Vitamin C.

Asparagine *See* Amino acids.

Atherosclerosis A buildup of fatty deposits (atheroma) within artery walls—a risk factor for heart disease, heart attack, and stroke.

Beta-carotene An antioxidant nutrient found in dark green, red, orange, and yellow fruits and vegetables, which is converted in the body to vitamin A.

Bile A bitter fluid produced by the liver, stored in the gall bladder, and released when required by the digestive process to break down fats and absorb vitamins.

Bioavailability The degree to which a substance, for example, a nutrient, is absorbed or becomes available to the body.

Biotin One of the B vitamins involved in the body's production of energy.

Blood sugar Refers to levels of sugar (glucose) in the blood, formed from digesting food and which the body uses for energy. Blood sugar levels are affected by the type of food consumed. High blood sugar levels are typical of people with diabetes.

Bowel The intestine, especially referring to the large intestine, concerned with the digestion and absorption of food.

Brassicas A family of edible plants, including broccoli, cabbage, cauliflower, kale, brussels sprouts, and radishes, believed to provide protection against various cancers. Also called cruciferous vegetables

Bromelain An enzyme found in pineapple, which is effective in treating blood clots, the cause of thrombosis.

Caffeine A naturally occurring and mildly addictive substance found in tea, coffee, cocoa, and cola drinks, which stimulates the central nervous system and heart and is a diuretic. Caffeine increases alertness, although, in excessive amounts, it can cause insomnia.

Calciferol Vitamin D.

Calories Strictly speaking kilocalories (abbreviated to kcal), these are units of energy values of foods.

Cancer Disease involving abnormal or uncontrolled growth of cells that can occur in any organ of the body.

243

Capsaicin An active compound in bell peppers and chilies.

Carbohydrate A major class of food comprising the sugars and starches found in grains and grain products (such as breads, rice), plus fruits and vegetables. Once digested, these turn into glucose, which is stored in the liver until required for energy.

Carcinogen Any cancer-triggering substance.

Cardiovascular disease
See Heart disease.

Carotenoid A group of powerful antioxidants, including alpha- and beta-carotene, responsible for the pigment of dark green, yellow, orange, and red fruits and vegetables. Many of the carotenoids convert to vitamin A in the body.

Chlorophyll The green pigment found in plants that traps the energy of the sun for photosynthesis.

Cholesterol A fatlike substance made by the body and carried in the blood. When blood cholesterol levels are too high, cholesterol may be deposited on the insides of blood vessels, thereby narrowing them and causing blockages, resulting in heart disease. There are two types of cholesterol: high-density lipoprotein (HDL), which is beneficial because it reduces blood cholesterol, and low-density lipoprotein (LDL), which is dangerous because it encourages cholesterol deposits in blood vessels.

Cobalamins Vitamin B_{12}, involved in the production of red blood cells and nerve cells.

Collagen Elastic protein that forms connective tissue in the body, for example, tendon, cartilage, and bone.
Colon The lower and largest part of the intestine, or bowel.

Cruciferous vegetables
See Brassicas.

Degenerative condition
A serious ailment that get worse with time.

Detoxification The process of removing toxins from the body, a buildup of which can contribute to ill health. The results of detoxifying include clearer skin, more regular bowel movements, and more efficient kidney and liver function.

Diabetes A disease caused by the body's inability to produce or properly use insulin, the hormone needed to convert sugar and other foods into energy. Diabetes complications include heart disease, blindness, and kidney disease. Diabetes can often be managed through lifestyle changes, including diet, and medication.

Diuretic A substance that causes an increase in urine production, dehydrating the body.

DNA Deoxyribonucleic acid, the genetic material in the body's cells that carries information on cell growth, division, and function.

Dopamine A chemical found in the brain that is an important neurotransmitter.

DRI *see* RDA

Ellagic acid A flavonoid believed to deplete cancer-causing substances in the body.

Empty calories A term used for food, such as alcohol and refined sugar, which contain calories but no nutrients.

Enzyme Protein substances involved in every chemical reaction in the body, for example, digestive enzymes are responsible for the digestion and absorption of food into the body.

Estrogen Group of hormones present in both men and women, but involved mainly with the female reproductive system.

Fats Vital in the diet for maintaining healthy skin and hair, regulating cholesterol, absorbing fat-soluble vitamins, promoting healthy cell function, and providing energy. Fats are generally classified as saturated, monounsaturated, or polyunsaturated. The food we eat contains varying proportions of these fats.

Fiber, dietary The indigestible parts of plant foods, which pass through the digestive system, absorbing water and accelerating waste elimination. Fiber helps keep the digestive system healthy, and regulates cholesterol and blood sugar levels, reducing the risk of bowel cancer, heart disease, and diabetes.

Flavonoids/bioflavonoids A group of antioxidant plant pigments, including flavones and flavanones, which work in synergy with vitamin C, neutralizing free radicals and helping reduce the risk of cancer.

Folate A B vitamin, also known as folic acid, required for the formation of red blood cells and for supporting the nervous system. A deficiency of folate in a woman before conceiving or during early pregnancy can cause anemia in the mom-to-be and neural tube defects in the baby. Folate also helps protect the heart by preventing buildup of homocysteine.

Folic acid *See* Folate.

Fortified foods Foods that have had nutrients added to them to benefit health, for example, bread fortified with selenium and breakfast cereals fortified with calcium and folate.

Free radicals Abnormal, electrochemically imbalanced molecules produced by the body as a natural waste product. They can set off a damaging chain reaction of oxidation within the body, resulting in wrinkles, sagging skin, age spots, and the onset of age-related diseases. The damage may be repaired by antioxidants.

Functional foods Foods with health-promoting or disease-preventing properties and for which a health claim has been authorized.

Gastrointestinal The complete digestive system.

Glucose The major sugar in the body and a key energy provider.

Glucosinolates Sulfurous organic compounds, for example sulforaphane, found in brassicas and believed to help prevent a variety of cancers.

Glutamine *See* Amino acids.

Glutathiones Water-soluble antioxidant found in the body, which can destroy toxins, such as carcinogens.

Glycaemic index A system rating the effect of carbohydrate-rich foods on blood sugar levels two hours after consumption. Foods with a low GI release glucose slowly into the bloodstream, which is better for energy provision and blood sugar levels.

Heart attack Any sudden severe instance of abnormal heart functioning, often caused by a sudden decrease in blood supply to the heart and resulting in chest pain.

Heart disease Also known as cardiovascular disease, this covers a range of problems affecting the heart and blood vessels, including atherosclerosis, coronary artery disease, angina, heart failure, and high blood pressure.

Hemoglobin The iron-containing protein molecule in red blood cells, responsible for the red color of blood.

Herperidin A flavonoid, also known as hesperidin, found in citrus fruits.

High blood pressure
Blood pressure is the force of blood against artery walls. High blood pressure, also known as hypertension, is a condition in which arterial blood pressure is persistently raised. It can lead to strokes, heart attacks, heart disease, and kidney failure. Diet plays a large role in both preventing and managing the condition.

Homocysteine An amino acid found in the blood. Folate can help lower raised homocysteine levels, which are associated with an increased risk of heart disease.

Hormones Chemical messengers produced and released within the body in tiny amounts and which circulate in the bloodstream. Imbalances can cause conditions such as diabetes.

Hydrogenation The chemical process of turning unsaturated liquid fat (vegetable oil) into solid or semisolid fat (margarine).

Hypertension
See High blood pressure.

Hypotension Abnormally low blood pressure.

Immune system The body's defense system, composed mainly of antibodies and white blood cells, which works to resist infection.

Insulin A hormone used to store glucose (sugar) and help regulate its concentration in the blood. Diabetics either can't produce adequate amounts of insulin or they can't use it efficiently and, therefore, have abnormal blood sugar levels.

Isoflavones A type of phytoestrogen found in soya beans and soy products, which may reduce menopausal symptoms and may be useful in treating cancer.

Isothiocyanates Beneficial phytonutrients responsible for the intense "heat" in plants such as horseradish, radishes, and mustards.

Kaempferol A flavonoid found in almonds, cranberries, strawberries, and peas.

Kidney stones Deposits of calcium salts in the kidneys that can cause pain and infection.

Lactobacillus *See* Probiotics.

Leucine *See* Amino acids.

Lignans Type of phytoestrogen found in flaxseed, whole-grains, and various fruits and vegetables, which may lower cholesterol, thereby protecting against heart disease and some cancers.

Linoleic acid An omega-6 essential fatty acid, vital for the body's health. Along with alpha-linoleic acid, one of the two main dietary polyunsaturated fatty acids.

Lutein A type of carotenoid which, like zeaxanthin, promotes healthy eyes, reducing the risk of cataracts and age-related macular degeneration.

Lycopene A carotenoid that reduces the risk of cancer, heart disease, and age-related eye problems. It is found in red fruits and vegetables and is particularly available in processed tomato products, such as canned tomatoes and tomato paste.

Lysine *See* Amino acids.

Macular degeneration Progressively poor vision due to degenerating blood supply to the retina. A common cause of blindness in the elderly.

Melatonin A hormone produced in the brain's pineal gland involved in regulating sleep and maintaining the body's natural time clock.

Metabolism All the biochemical processes that occur within the body by which it survives, grows, produces energy, and eliminates waste, for example, breathing, blood circulation, and digestion.

Minerals Inorganic elements essential for normal body function and good health. Some minerals are essential components in the body; for example, calcium in bones and iron in the blood's hemoglobin. Others help regulate metabolic processes.

Monounsaturated fat Fatty acids found in nuts, avocados, and olive oil, which help maintain healthy cholesterol levels and are, therefore, thought to protect against heart disease.

Naringin A bitter-tasting flavonoid compound.

Nervous system The body's network of specialized cells, including the brain, which transmit nerve impulses around the body.

Neural tube defects Malformation of the brain or spinal cord (neurological system) during development in the womb. A good intake of folate by women before conception and during early pregnancy greatly reduces the risk to the baby.

Neurotransmitters
Biochemical messengers that enable nerves in the brain to communicate.

Niacin Vitamin B_3, one of the B vitamins involved in the body's production of energy.

Nitrosamines Carcinogenic chemical compounds found in certain processed foods.

Nutraceuticals
See Functional foods.

Nutrient density Nutrient dense foods provide substantial amounts of vitamins and minerals relative to their calorie content. Calorie-dense foods supply calories yet relatively few nutrients.

Omega-3 Essential fatty acids (EFAs) that must be acquired from the diet. Found in oily fish, walnuts,

and flaxseed, omega-3s help reduce the risk of heart disease, improve mental function, and deal with joint pain. Most people need to include more omega-3s in their diets.

Omega-6 Essential fatty acids (EFAs) that must be acquired from the diet, found in corn and sunflower oils, nuts, and seeds. Many people in modern industrialized societies are actually consuming too many omega-6 fats (from polyunsaturated margarines and oils, often "hidden" in manufactured baked goods) at the expense of omega-3s.

ORAC Oxygen Radical Absorbance Capacity, a test developed at the Human Nutrition Research Center on Aging at Tufts University, Boston, MA, to determine the antioxidant power of different foods.

Organic foods Organic fruits and vegetables grown without the use of synthetic pesticides, fertilizers, or fungicides. Organic

meat comes from animals raised without routine antibiotics or growth hormones.

Osteoporosis Skeletal disease caused by loss of bone density. The bones become fragile and prone to fracture. Osteoporosis is more common in women, especially after the menopause, and often goes undetected until a fracture occurs. A good calcium intake during childhood, adolescence, and early adulthood, plus regular weight-bearing exercise can help prevent the disease from occurring.

Oxalic acid A substance found in certain foods, for example, spinach, which is poisonous in excessive amounts. Anyone with kidney or bladder stones should avoid foods containing oxalic acid because it can aggravate these conditions.

Oxidization Oxidative damage to the cells of the body ("rusting"), due to the action of unstable, unpaired free radicals, which take a hydrogen ion from nearby molecules to "pair off." These newly unpaired molecules then do the same thing, setting up a chain reaction within the body that leads to tissue damage but can be stopped by antioxidants.

Pantothenic acid Vitamin B_5, one of the B vitamins involved in the body's production of energy.

Papain An enzyme found in papayas, which helps in the digestion of protein.

Pectin A soluble fiber found in the pith and cellular membranes of many ripe fruits and vegetables. It helps maintain bowel function and lower blood cholesterol levels.

Phytochemicals
See Phytonutrients.

Phytoestrogens Substances found in plants that are similar to human estrogens. They are thought to help reduce some of the symptoms of premenstrual syndrome and the menopause.

Phytonutrients Plant chemicals at the forefront of scientific research into food and health and of interest for their role in preventing serious diseases, such as cancer, heart disease, asthma, and arthritis.

Polyunsaturated fat
Fatty acids that are usually liquid at room temperature, for example, vegetable oils, and can be converted to trans fats by hydrogenation.

Precursor A biochemical substance, from which another more definitive product is formed.

Proanthocyanidins
Type of tannin found in cranberries, cocoa, and chocolate, believed to help improve urinary tract health and reduce the risk of heart disease.

Probiotics Live microorganisms, for example, *lactobacilli* and *bifidobacteria,* which are added to foods, such as yogurt, to improve gastrointestinal health.

Protein A complex compound formed from nitrogen and amino acids, which is required in the diet by our bodies for growth and repair. Proteins are found mainly in animal products, as well as in grains and legumes.

Provitamin A substance that can be converted via the body's normal metabolic processes into a vitamin. Carotene, for example, is a provitamin of vitamin A.

Pterostilbene An antioxidant compound found in blueberries and grapes.

Purines Natural substances found in virtually all foods and useful in the body. High-purine foods such as organ meat, anchovies, and sardines, should be avoided by people with gout since purines are broken down into uric acid, an accumulation of which is responsible for gout.

Pyridoxine Vitamin B_6, essential for many processes within the body, including the formation of new cells (including red blood and nerve cells), the production of energy, and balancing hormonal changes in women.

Quercetin A flavonoid with anti-inflammatory and anticancer properties, found in the skins of apples and red onions.

249

RDA Recommended Daily/ Dietary Allowance, the level of intake of specific vitamins and minerals recommended each day to maintain good health. The United States now uses DRIs (Dietry Reference Intakes), replacing RDAs. Great Britain relies on DRVs (Dietary Reference Values), and the European Union has PRIs (Population Reference Intakes).

Red blood cells Blood cells containing hemoglobin, which carry oxygen to and from body tissues and organs. Lack of red blood cells can cause fatigue and anemia.

Resveratrol A flavonoid with both antioxidant and anti-inflammatory properties, found mainly in red wine.

Retinol Vitamin A.

Riboflavin VAlso known as Vitamin B$_2$, one of the B vitamins involved in the body's production of energy.

Rutin A citrus flavonoid that works well with vitamin C. Found in buckwheat and many fruits.

Salicylates Naturally occurring aspirin-like compounds found in certain foods, for example, almonds, strawberries, and tomatoes.

Saponins Phytonutrients found in soy beans and soy products, which may lower LDL cholesterol and help protect against cancer.

Saturated fat A fat of animal origin (with the exception of palm oil and coconut oil), which is solid at room temperature. Too much saturated fat in the diet raises blood cholesterol and increases the risk of heart disease.

Serotonin A neurotransmitter that helps regulate sleep patterns and mood. Low levels of serotonin are associated with depression.

Starchy foods Carbohydate foods with a high content of starch, for example, bread, rice, pasta, and potatoes.

Stroke A brain injury caused by disrupted blood supply to the brain via the cerebral arteries—in the same way that blocked arteries to the heart can cause heart attack.

Sulforaphane A powerful compound found in brassicas that is effective in removing carcinogens from the body.

Super foods Foods with alleged healing or health-promoting capabilities, also referred to as "miracle foods."

Synergy Two or more substances working in tandem to synergistic effect, whereby they achieve more in partnership than either could alone.

Tannin Antioxidant substance found in grape seeds, red wine, and tea. Too much tannin reduces the body's ability to absorb iron.

Thiamin Vitamin B$_1$, one of the B vitamins involved in the body's production of energy. Occurs in the outer coat of rice and other grains.

Tocopherol Vitamin E.

Toxins Harmful substances that may be consumed in food or created by the body as a waste product and need to be eliminated.

Trans fats Damaging type of fat produced during the hydrogenation process of turning unsaturated liquid fat (vegetable oils) into solid fat (margarine). High consumption of trans fats raises blood cholesterol and increases the risk of heart disease.

Tryptophan One of the essential amino acids. A component of proteins needed by the body for growth and a precursor of both serotonin and niacin.

Tyrosine *See* Amino acids.

Ultraviolet UV, an invisible band of radiation at the upper end of the visible light spectrum. Too much exposure to the sun's UV rays can damage the eyes, immune system, and skin and can cause skin cancers, such as melanoma.

Unsaturated fat Group of fatty acids encompassing monounsaturated, polyunsaturated fats and the two essential fatty acids the body cannot make for itself, linoleic acid (omega-6) and alpha-linolenic acid (omega-3). Relatively healthy fats, which help reduce levels of blood cholesterol.

Uric acid A natural waste product derived from the breakdown of purines and usually eliminated from the body in the urine. Abnormal buildup of uric acid crystals in the body may result in gout, a painful condition in which certain joints become inflamed.

Vitamins Organic compounds required by the body in small quantities for normal health and development. There are two main types: fat-soluble vitamins (A, D, E, and K), which are stored in the body, and water-soluble ones (vitamin C and the B complex vitamins). The latter are not stored in the body and are required on a daily basis from food in the diet or via supplements.

White blood cells Large blood cells that are part of the immune system and help the body fight foreign invaders and infections.

Whole grains Largely unprocessed nutrient-rich grain foods (for example whole or rolled oats, whole wheat, bulgur, or brown rice) that provide the maximum health benefits.

Zeaxanthin A type of carotenoid that, like lutein, promotes healthy eyes, reducing the risk of cataracts and age-related macular degeneration.

252

index

256

acknowledgements

Executive Editor Nicola Hill
Editor Lisa John
Design Manager Tokiko Morishima
Designer Jo MacGregor
Home Economist Mary Wall
Senior Production Controller Manjit Sihra

Special Photography © **Octopus Publishing Group Limited**/Stephen Conroy.
Other Photography © **Octopus Publishing Group Limited**/Jeremy Hopley 165,
223, 231; William Lingwood 106, 180, 197, 205.